Blueprint *for a* Lasting Marriage

THE COMPLETE GUIDE TO BUILDING YOUR HAPPILY EVER AFTER WITH MORE INTENTION, LESS WORK

Lesli Doares, M.S., LMFT

Femme Osage Publishing
St. Peters, Missouri

Femme Osage Publishing
7127 Mexico Road, Suite 121
St. Peters, MO 63376
636-922-2634

ISBN 978-1-934509-36-4
Library of Congress Control # 2010942282

*Names and identifying characteristics of people in the book
have been changed to protect the privacy of the individuals.*

*The information in this book is not a substitute for the
services of a professional counselor or therapist.*

Editing by Marian Sandmaier
Book design by Sara Patton
Printed in the United States

For information on bulk sales of this book
contact Lesli Doares
www.blueprintforalastingmarriage.com
or sales@vervante.com

CONTENTS

To Esteban, my best friend and biggest cheerleader. You inspire me to be my best self. Everything I am or will be is because you came into my life. Thank you for your love.

The secret to having a good marriage is to understand that marriage must be total, it must be permanent, and it must be equal.

– Frank Pittman, psychiatrist
and family therapy pioneer

INTRODUCTION

I remember my 15th birthday like it was yesterday. You see, birthdays in my family had always been special occasions. The birthday child got to choose a special dinner menu and my mom would make the requested flavor of cake. But things didn't quite go as usual the day I turned 15. Instead of the savory lamb dish I always requested, my "special" meal was leftover chili. There also was no birthday cake.

Just a few days before, my father left for the final time. But on my birthday, he called to say he was coming to bring me a present. My mother shut herself up in her room so she wouldn't have to see him. My oldest sister was in the kitchen slamming my father with words as she was furiously slamming the cupboard doors. My middle sister was in tears in the front yard, and my brother was stuck in his room in his wheelchair dealing with his own sorrow. I sat alone on the orange and green flecked couch I had always hated with my family in ruins. I said quietly to myself, "Happy Birthday, Lesli." It was the first of many times I would experience the pain that a divorce can bring to what should be special, happy events. It also shadowed my view of relationships, and my behavior in them, for many years to come.

My journey to becoming a therapist was not straightforward, but I do believe it was inevitable. I was a shy child when I was very young and spent much of my time watching people and trying to figure out what they were doing and why. Instead of playing with my classmates, I would sit on the sidelines and just watch. In fact I even got an "unsatisfactory" in kindergarten because I wouldn't play with the other kids at recess. I also paid very close attention to the personal dynamics that were playing out in my family as I was growing up. Being the third of three girls with less than three years separating oldest and youngest, and having a brother six years younger, provided me a certain vantage point that bordered on invisibility.

I suppose it was a typical middle-class existence in the early 1960s, one that did not seem terribly different from that of my friends. That is until my brother, on whom my father had placed all his hopes and dreams, was diagnosed with cerebral palsy. I was eight and the security of my world began to crumble. My father began spending more time at the office. Family vacations became my mother and the children; Dad couldn't get away. My dad would leave, come back, and leave again.

The day he told us he was leaving for good was the first time I saw my father cry. He gathered the four of us around the kitchen table and told us he would no longer be living in our house. My father had always seemed so strong and capable, but on that day he struggled to find the words he didn't want to say, and I didn't want to hear. I remember thinking it was my fault. If I could only have kept from arguing with my middle sister all the time my dad wouldn't be leaving. It was a moment that changed my life forever and would return to haunt me from time to time.

When I met the man who would become my husband I was living in Southern California, where I was born and raised. Steve was in graduate school and his program was moving to Athens, Georgia, clear on the other side of way beyond. He asked me if I would consider moving with him. I responded that I would, only if I had a ring on my left hand. He proposed and we moved to a place where I knew no one and felt lost in a world of "yes, ma'ams" and "y'alls."

On my first day on the job at one of the best department stores in Atlanta, I met Jessica. We were the same age and both engaged. In fact, her wedding day was exactly six months to the day before mine. The shoes she wore for her wedding became the something borrowed at mine. Jessica helped me navigate my new job. But most of all she helped me with my transition to the South. She even taught me to eat grits by revealing the taste-enhancing magic that quantities of butter and melted cheese impart.

Jessica and her husband Eric became our good friends, and we felt secure in our own and our collective happiness. We began a tradition of spending New Year's Eve together and welcoming in what we were sure would be another wonderful year. Then, after five years in Athens, my husband and I again moved across the country, this time to the state of Washington. The following New Year's Eve day, Steve and I were surprised to receive a phone call in the middle of the afternoon. It was Eric. We assumed he was calling to wish us the usual "Happy New Year." Instead, he said quietly, "Jessica has left me."

My heart dropped to my stomach and my knees gave out. It took all the strength I had just to hold onto the phone. I have no idea what else Eric said or how the conversation came to an end. I just knew that all my insecurities about marriage left over from my parents' divorce, which had lain dormant for years, suddenly sprang to life. The first of my friends' divorces was on the books. What had gone wrong for Jessica and Eric? Could the same thing happen to me? Was there anything I could do to avoid that same fate?

Intent on better understanding how marriages fail—and how they might succeed instead—I began to study to be a psychotherapist. My first practical experience doing therapy was in a local domestic violence shelter. I learned firsthand just how badly relationships can get off track. I saw real bruises on my clients' faces, as well as the deeper emotional wounds reflected in their eyes. I watched as these women tried to remake themselves into the perfect partners, only to fall short again and again. Their unshakable belief that their failing relationship was their own fault, and therefore it was solely up to them to fix it, led me to wonder what my clients had been taught about love and intimate relationships.

I became a licensed marriage and family therapist, went into private practice, and began to see couples every day. Like Jessica and Eric, most of these couples had been in love on their wedding day. But it was clear that love was not enough. If love were all that were needed for a successful marriage, the failure rate would not be 50%. Far too many marriages crashed and burned, and I came to understand that it had little to do with marrying the "wrong" person. For most troubled couples, problems developed because the relationships slowly and imperceptibly ended up taking second place to other concerns of life—work, kids, self-improvement, or the household problem of the moment. As I saw more and more couples, it became clear to me that most of them sought support for their relationship only when they were in crisis and on the verge of divorce. On average, their distress and pain had been going on for five to seven years. At this point, the task became one of undoing damage and trying to rebuild a positive connection. Often, it was too late for that.

Later, when we finally had the chance to talk, Jessica told me what had gone wrong for her and Eric. When they first got together, Eric was extremely aware and concerned about Jessica's happiness. He was from a small town and thought he had hit the jackpot when he met someone as sophisticated and classy as Jessica. He paid attention to the things she liked to do because he was so intent on making a good impression. But, Eric and Jessica were like many couples in the early years of marriage. They were young and smart and worked hard at building their careers. Jessica was moving up the ladder in the retail industry. Eric was trying to make his name in the world of corporate finance. The romantic dinners and carefully planned dates Eric made such an effort to arrange fell by the wayside, lost to lack of time and attention. By the time the marriage ended, they simply existed in the same space but had no real idea what the other was thinking or feeling. The only time they spent together was when they were restoring the house they had recently purchased. Eric felt pressure to keep advancing in his job to provide Jessica with the creature comforts she had grown up with. Jessica felt she had been sold a bill of goods as the romantic man she fell in love with spent less and less time with her. It got to the point where Jessica and Eric grew too far apart for them to be able to bridge the distance. Many years later Eric shared with me that his mom was a drug addict, and that his father was the son of an alcoholic. "I just didn't have the skills at the time and didn't develop them fully until years later after I'd spent time in therapy and Al-Anon. In retrospect, Jessica and I never had a chance."

What I have learned from Jessica and Eric's story, and many more like theirs, is that marriage is not a singular accomplishment. It is a living, growing thing that requires daily nurturing in order to thrive. The problem is that most of us don't have a clue how to create a committed, thriving marriage. There is a lot of information out there on how to find your soulmate and then on planning the perfect wedding once you do. There are also bookshelves full of remedies once your relationship gets in trouble. What seems to be missing is a practical understanding of how to keep the joy of your wedding day alive and well, day by day.

This book will provide you and your partner with the tools to nurture your marriage. While couples contemplating marriage can certainly benefit, I wrote this book for couples in their first year of marriage as they navigate this major life transition. It may also be beneficial for couples who have been married for a while but may have forgotten—or perhaps never had the chance to learn— how to keep their marriage healthy and growing. My mission is to help couples like you and your partner hold onto the love and trust that led you to commit to each other in the first place. I hope to be your marriage mentor, not just your marriage mender. Providing couples with the knowledge and tools necessary to nurture their relationship right from the beginning and keep it strong and healthy through the years is the aim of this book.

You might well wonder why I would write a book for couples on how to create their own happily-ever-after with stories of failed or failing marriages. The answer is quite simple really. If you know what it takes to create and sustain a thriving marriage then divorce can be something that happens to other people. In addition, no child of yours will ever suffer the kind of loss and aloneness that I felt—and so many millions of children feel—in the wake of a shattered marriage. Instead, you and your partner can build the successful and satisfying marriage you both hoped for when you fell in love.

CHAPTER 1
WHY YOU NEED A BLUEPRINT

All weddings are similar,
but every marriage is different.

– John Berger, novelist

Congratulations on your marriage! You have found your life's partner and celebrated your commitment with your friends and family. It was a day filled with joy and the promise of a new beginning. You and your partner have embarked on the journey of joining your two lives into one. Hopefully, the transition is going relatively smoothly. You and your partner may have already successfully negotiated some of the mundane tasks of married life. You may be finding more of a challenge in other areas. How you handle this major life transition now will have a major impact on the long-term success and happiness of your marriage. Using the information provided in this book can help to smooth the bumps couples can encounter during this critical stage in their relationship.

Marriage is a commitment couples make with love and hope for a happy life together. Managing that commitment on a daily basis is where the challenge comes in. Understanding what's involved, and committing to those behaviors, is what will allow your marriage to not only survive, but thrive. It will also enable you and your partner to avoid some common mistakes that lead many couples to give up on their relationships in the mistaken belief that marriage is an antiquated concept with no place in today's modern world.

Recently, I overheard a conversation between a life coach and a man contemplating a business that would offer marriage insurance. The life coach openly questioned the idea. "Marriage doesn't work," she stated flatly. Based on the evidence that people marrying today have about a 50% chance of divorce, one might conclude that she is right. However, to paraphrase Winston Churchill, marriage is the worst form of relationship, except for all those other forms that have been tried from time to time.

What is it about marriage today that makes it so difficult to maintain a happy and successful union? And if marriages are doomed to fail, why do people keep trying? To answer these questions, it is important to consider why you and many other people continue to marry.

MARRIAGE TODAY

Marriage in one form or another has been around since people have been living in organized groups. Every society has found a way to formalize this intimate coupling that encompasses societal, economic, emotional, spiritual, and civil aspects of life. Marriage has been the formal means of sustaining families, protecting property, and cementing the ties between families, tribes, and nations.

But the institution of marriage has changed in many ways over time. One hundred years ago life expectancy was only about 47 years. Even if people got married at age 20, "until death do us part" meant something very different than it does today. Life was often difficult and focus was on the necessity to survive and to provide the economic resources to raise children to adulthood rather than on the happiness of the couple. Even if a marriage was very unhappy, it was difficult to leave it. Divorce was a rare and socially unacceptable option.

Social revolution arrived in the 1960s and 1970s, with women's liberation and the sexual revolution. Whereas marriage previously had been predictable and the roles of each spouse clearly defined, it now became a function of individual choice and personal happiness. For many women, financial dependence is no longer a reason to remain in a relationship they find unfulfilling. Likewise, the role of breadwinner is no longer a sufficient one for many married men. Now, both men and women are looking for emotional support, a sense of personal fulfillment, and an ongoing intimate connection with their life partner.

THE CHOICE TO STAY MARRIED

Today, marriage is a choice, not an expectation or a necessity. For some, it's a decision based on comfort and dependability. For others, it's a commitment to something greater than one's own individual needs or happiness. But whatever it is, your marriage is no longer constrained by the rules of the past. Each and every day, you and your partner must decide whether—and why—it is worthwhile to stay married. This makes your marriage both precious and fragile. It also makes the choice of who, when, and how to marry one of the most important any of us will ever make. It is a decision that should be made with great care and deliberation. Unfortunately, it is one frequently made in the heat of passion.

People are full of contradictions. We want the safety, security, and comfort of a committed relationship as well as the breathless, swept-off-one's-feet exhilaration of being in love. How often have you heard that someone loves somebody but is no longer "in love" with them? Do you truly believe there is a difference between loving your partner and being "in love" with them? Is it possible to fall in love *and* stay in love with your partner? I believe it is. But first, we must understand the process of attraction and love.

When you fall in love the world looks and feels different. The sun shines more brightly, colors are more vivid, food tastes better, and everything is more intense. You can stay up all night and still have energy to burn. Your every waking moment is focused on that special someone. You feel both out of control and captivated by the wild ride and have no intention of getting off. It is as though you have found the perfect drug—and, in a way, you have.

Falling in love *does* involve being high on drugs, but these drugs are *naturally* produced by the body. When we become attracted to someone, and start to fall in love, our brain releases two neurotransmitters: dopamine and norepinephrine. These natural chemicals are responsible for our bright outlook, our increased energy levels, and our sharpened sense of perception. Phenylethylamine (PEA) is also released when we are with the one we love. This neurotransmitter gives us a sense of comfort and security. When we are separated from that special someone our levels of PEA drop sharply, causing a crash in mood and the onset of withdrawal symptoms. This withdrawal is commonly known as love sickness.

This intoxicating stage of love also includes a strong psychological component. You view your new love as perfect. This person knows and meets all your needs without your needing to ask. Your partner is the solution to all of your emotional problems and will heal all childhood wounds. Their love will make you whole and happy. As we often hear, this new love will "complete" you.

When my client Karen first met Mark, she fell for him hard and fast. He was tall, strong, and confident, but also very sensitive. He could bench press 300 pounds *and* cry at the end of *Casablanca*, Karen's favorite movie. Mark paid attention to the little things Karen would mention and surprise her with a related item on their next date. Once, she was reading a recipe for crab cakes in the newspaper and mentioned to Mark how good they sounded. The very next weekend he swept her away for a weekend in Baltimore with dinner at a restaurant famous for its crab cakes. In Karen's eyes, Mark was perfect. By this she meant that he was nothing like her father.

Karen's father was cold and distant. When she was growing up, he was always working and rarely showed up for occasions that were important to Karen. On the night of her high school graduation, she cried herself to sleep because he was not there. He never paid attention to anything she requested, whether it was the chance to participate in activities like soccer and dance or a request for a special birthday or Christmas present. Karen learned that asking for anything was a waste of time and energy. She also absorbed the message that she was both unimportant and invisible.

Mark changed all that for Karen. She blossomed under his attention and care. Three months after they met, they were engaged. On the anniversary of their first date, they got married. A year after the wedding, Karen was sitting in my office, devastated by her conviction that Mark didn't love her anymore and that the marriage had been a horrible mistake.

Trying to understand Karen's words between sobs, I learned that her distress had been set off by Mark being called away on an unexpected business trip two days before their anniversary. He had been able to postpone their planned romantic getaway to the next month, but that didn't comfort Karen. Her belief that Mark was truly different from her father, and that she was finally a priority to someone, hung by a thread.

Karen's story is a familiar one. Nothing is essentially wrong between her and Mark. It is simply that the top-of-the-world euphoria Karen shared with Mark has crashed—as it must for everyone. Usually within six months of falling in love, levels of the "passion drugs" in your system begin to wane and the fantasies of the perfection of your relationship yield to the reality of human frailty. You discover you would rather have a good night's sleep the night before a big presentation at work than stay up chatting online until 3 a.m. with your special someone. The cute way your partner would be 15 minutes early because they wanted to see you is now making you feel pressed for time. By the time 18 to 36 months go by, you are no longer "in love." The initial surge of attraction and exhilaration that you experienced is an evolutionary strategy designed to ensure the survival of the species. The time allotted to being in love is long enough to meet, mate, and procreate. Marriage is not essential to this physiological perspective.

> **To be successful for the long term, you need to develop a more committed relationship, one that is consciously created if it is to last.**

However, like Mark and Karen, many couples decide to get married during this euphoric stage. To be successful for the long term, you and your partner now need to develop a more committed relationship. This new relationship must be consciously created if it is to last. It will be more satisfying than the one you experienced in the first blush of love. This relationship is one that is founded on the promises you both make to build a life together. It includes consideration of your partner at all levels. It is one that provides an overall sense of security and acceptance, that provides shelter from the difficulties life may throw at you. This relationship also must be based in the reality of who the two of you actually are, not who you need each other to be. This means you need to be clear about what you expect from your partner and from the relationship itself.

THE POWER OF EXPECTATIONS

The issue of expectations around marriage is exceedingly important to its success. Mary Elizabeth Hughes, a sociology professor at Johns Hopkins University, tells us in "A Nation Divided by Images of Wedlock" that marriage has changed from an expected social institution to one of a voluntary lifestyle choice based on self-fulfillment. According to her, there is an increased emphasis on being established before getting married. David Brooks, a columnist for the *New York Times,* agrees, observing that our society views marriage as the pinnacle of adult life instead of one of its foundations. He notes that marriage is now viewed as a sacred state that cannot be attempted unless the conditions are perfect. He states that people "don't want to marry until they are financially secure and emotionally mature. They don't want to marry until they can afford to have a white-dress wedding and time to plan it. They don't want to marry until they are absolutely sure they can trust the person they are with."

On the other hand, there is the view represented in the movie *Jerry McGuire* of needing a partner to be emotionally complete. Jerry McGuire is a self-centered sports agent who doesn't even notice his secretary, a single mother, until he loses his job. He starts dating her because she is the only one who stays with him after he's fired. She has secretly been in love with him for years and believes he has finally seen the light and returns her love. In her mind, her life is now complete. This perspective of marriage includes partner as soulmate and source of happiness. The expectation is one of always being in love, always happy, and always together. If you can be certain you have found "the right one," any existing problems magically disappear on the day of the wedding and love will keep them away. It is the idea that your partner will embrace your way of thinking and behaving once the ring is on your finger because love is unconditional and can conquer all.

The problem with both of these approaches is that they are based on unrealistic expectations. The idea that you can only be "complete" and happy in the presence of a partner implies you have limited control over your own life. The power of your emotional well-being lies in someone else's hands and you must simply sit on the sidelines waiting to be swept off your feet. Hughes and Brookes take the opposite position: that you must be completely settled in your own life with all your i's dotted and t's crossed before you can even consider marriage. Their position also implies a confidence that, because you have your life in order, you can know all there is to know about your partner, and how the two of you will be together over time, before you marry. So one position puts all the responsibility for a successful marriage on your partner, and the other assumes you have total control over a relationship that intimately involves another person. The reality is somewhere in between. You do have to be able to take care of yourself financially and emotionally before you can join your life with someone else's. However, there is no "perfect" time for marriage. There is no guarantee of success in marriage because you can manage your own life. This is because you can only grow so far on your own. Part of what helps us to grow and mature is learning how to accommodate another person's needs and desires, not just focusing on our own. This process of learning to merge your two lives into one will be addressed throughout this book.

The further expectations are from reality, the greater the disappointment when things don't go as planned.

I have discovered over the course of my practice that the further expectations are from reality, the greater the disappointment when things don't go as planned. Marriage becomes a fragile entity when too many demands are placed on the relationship. It is colored by habits, expectations, and unspoken understandings of how married people are supposed to act. When it falls short of that blissful dream, as in Karen and Mark's case, it can result in deep hurt and anger and the conclusion that one's partner wasn't who they purported to be or didn't really love you the way you believed. What is rarely examined is whether any relationship can hold up to the unreasonable burdens being placed on it.

Marriage is a living entity that grows and changes with time and circumstance. Your marriage must be allowed to have both the flexibility and the strength to respond to the changes that life brings. If it doesn't, it will either become brittle, shattering into pieces, or it will become stagnant, unable to adapt to the challenges of life. The expectations you and your partner bring to your relationship will determine the path it takes. Because of the importance of these pre-existing conditions, it is important to have a clear understanding of your ideas about marriage and where they come from. Be sure your partner understands their own expectations too. The more honest both of you can be about your ideas and hopes about marriage, the greater the chance you have for a successful marriage.

MARRIAGE MYTHS

Unrealistic expectations sometimes expand into full-fledged "marriage myths" that can be enormously persuasive. The first of these myths is the idea of a SOULMATE: the idea that there is one person who, if you could just find them, would bring eternal love and happiness to your life. This person would be able to read your mind and fulfill all of your dreams without requiring any input from you. They would anticipate your every need and desire and have it filled before you even knew it existed. Like Karen, you might think you have found that person during your "in love" phase. It makes sense to you, because your new love is paying a lot of attention to you and your needs. You feel as though you are the center of your partner's universe and, in a way, it's true. The problem is in believing, or expecting, that it's *always* going to be that way.

In a healthy marriage, you need to find a healthy balance between your needs and those of your partner. This change in focus doesn't mean that your partner isn't right for you, or that they don't love you anymore. It just means your relationship is in a different developmental stage, a more mature and realistic one. Your partner hasn't changed. What has changed, quite naturally and inevitably, is just the intensity of the relationship.

This expectation of a perfectly attuned soulmate leads to the second myth that MARRIAGE IS ALL ABOUT YOU AND YOUR HAPPINESS. Unfortunately, this is a common view about marriage today. We constantly hear that life is too short to waste time being discontented. This sets up a sense of entitlement based on the idea that we have the right to be happy all the time and in all aspects of our lives. Not only is it okay to consider abandoning a relationship that displeases you for any length of time, it is practically a requirement. However, the marriage vows most people take emphasize staying together for "better or worse" until death, not for as long as you feel good. (Please note, this does not mean you should silently make do in a relationship if you are truly suffering. There are very valid reasons, such as abuse or unaddressed addiction, for leaving a marriage. What I am addressing here is the commonly accepted perception that being temporarily unhappy or uncomfortable in a relationship is a sufficient justification for ending it.)

Marriage is about creating a life with another person. Your part in this endeavor is being open and honest about what you want that life to look like and then doing your part to make it happen. So if you want to live in a certain place or have a specific number of children, it is up to you to bring these wishes to your partner and work through any disparities that might be present. Your partner will have the same responsibility, so sometimes this means the conversation will be about your life view, and sometimes it will be about your partner's. How well you come to accept this will play a big role in the success of your relationship. If you follow the adage that it is better to give than to receive, you can choose to be happy when the focus is on your partner. In reality, this generosity is just an extension of the attention you probably bestowed on your partner during the time you were "in love." You extended yourself freely and happily to your partner then. Doing the same now will result in the same feeling of contentment.

The third myth is that **LOVE CAN CONQUER ALL**. Its corollary is *love is all you need* to be happily married. These twin myths persuade you that if you and your partner just love each other enough, your relationship can survive *anything*. Love may be a necessary component for marriage, but it is hardly sufficient. If love was really that powerful, half of all marriages would not end in divorce. Since most people are in love with each other on their wedding day, there must be other important ingredients for marital success. The strategy I will present during the course of this book defines those other elements necessary to build a strong, happy marriage.

The fourth myth of marriage is that **LOVE IS UNCONDITIONAL**. This is a comforting concept, but it just isn't true. If unconditional love exists, it is only as a parent's love for a child. It simply doesn't exist in a long-term, peer relationship such as marriage. How you are treated by your partner is going to influence your thoughts, feelings, and actions toward them, and vice versa. Love is a reciprocal emotion: the more you feel it, the more likely you will return it. Willard F. Harley, Jr., Ph.D., discusses "love units" and a "love bank" to express this idea in his book, *His Needs, Her Needs*. The overall feeling of love, safety, and security that is present in a relationship both determines and is determined by how the two people in that relationship treat each other. If your partner is meeting your needs, you are more likely to meet theirs, and vice versa.

Not getting your needs met, or not meeting your partner's, results in less love flowing through the system. You are then likely to stop looking for ways to make your partner happy and start focusing on what they have done for you lately—or failed to do. When this kind of marital scorekeeping gets underway, many partners fall out of love and start looking for a way out.

This process of not doing what you each promised to do for each other, and what you know to be the right way of being in a relationship, leads to justifications for your behavior. You begin to convince yourself that you have a right not to do loving things for your partner. Once you start this self-justifying behavior, your view of your relationship becomes distorted. You begin to pay attention to those things your partner does that support your position. This view of reality influences your behavior towards your partner, and not for the better. Since relationships function on a continual feed-back loop, what you put into the relationship is frequently what you will get in return. Choosing to pay attention only to the per-ceived negative behaviors of your partner sets your relationship up to fail. Your love, and loving behavior, for your partner has indeed become conditional.

The fifth myth is what I call the "FAIRY TALE FALLACY." You know the story: young woman with good heart meets the hand-some prince under mysterious circumstances. She finds herself in harm's way. The prince takes great risks to come to her rescue. They fall in love, marry, and, with no further effort, live happily ever after.

My friend Richard had bought into this idea. His second marriage to a very close friend of mine, Renee, ended about the same time that my marriage began. When they first got together Richard was very attentive and considerate. He used to cook dinner for Renee every weekend. Once he discovered scallops were her favorite food, he took great pleasure in finding new ways to fix them. He paid attention to the things she liked to do, such as going on picnics and attending antique auctions, and would look through the local papers to find places they could go. By the time the marriage ended, Richard had long abandoned such acts of generosity and was totally focused on what he wanted to do and how he wanted to live. Richard wanted to move up in his company and started to spend more time at work. He was offered an assignment in Southeast Asia that would last two years. Richard didn't understand why Renee was not as excited as he was. It never occurred to him that she would have to leave her job as well. Richard took the job anyway. He didn't feel any obligation to make decisions that would make the marriage work.

Like the prince in the fairy tale, he believed all the attention in a relationship needed to be on the front end, during the courtship phase. Once the "I do's" were said and the honeymoon was over, so was the attention and effort. Richard had won the prize and now he could go back to focusing on his own goals and desires. I vividly remember sitting on my front porch when he asked me if I thought he should get married for a third time. "Only if you still think there is a difference between marriage and courtship behavior with marriage behavior coming out on top this time," I replied. He looked surprised when I said this. I simply meant that for all the effort one puts into winning your partner, the real energy comes in actions that keep your relationship going. He must have heard me, because I'm happy to say that, this time around, he has been successfully married for over 15 years.

Taking the time and energy to define what you want your marriage to look like and carefully setting clear standards in place at the beginning minimizes the need for Herculean effort later.

The final myth I want to address is that **MARRIAGE IS WORK**. This is a commonly accepted myth that can doom a marriage to failure if it is taken at face value. A marriage based on honesty and founded on realistic expectations requires attention and intention to be successful, but it doesn't require drudgery over the long term. Taking the time and energy to define what you want your marriage to look like and carefully setting clear standards in place at the beginning minimizes the need for Herculean effort later.

Setting clear standards involves discussing all aspects of marriage—emotional, financial, domestic, familial, etc.—and becoming both aware of, and accepting of, each other's views. You understand that neither is responsible for the other's happiness, but you do try to bring out the best in each other. You recognize there will be bumps in the road but are committed to navigating those bumps together. You understand that marriage is about more than love, it's also about building a life together. If you can do all of this, and then pay conscious attention to the relationship and behave in *its* best interest, the concept of work won't enter the picture.

DESIGNING A MARRIAGE

Creating a lasting and fulfilling relationship with one person requires not only commitment, but also a certain level of tolerance for emotional anxiety. You cling to the notion of "being in love" because in that state you feel alive and connected to this special person. However, when you look to another to "complete" you, you lose your ability to stand on your own two feet. You cannot survive as a separate entity if you only feel whole in the presence of someone else. The ability to function as a separate being is what allows you to be truly connected to another. *You are not a couple because you fear being alone, but because you make a conscious choice to be together.*

This choice is what allows you to manage the normal anxiety

that arises when you and your partner disagree. Knowing how to handle your reaction during inevitable disagreements will keep you and your partner from avoiding them. It is natural to pull away when emotional confusion caused by these episodes is stirred up. However, actively recognizing your commitment to your partner, and acting in support of that commitment, frees you to move past your anxiety and resolve your differences. This focus on the promises you and your partner have made acts like a security blanket to calm your anxiety and allows both of you to concentrate on following your common life plan.

A successful relationship requires you to love and honor your partner and put their needs and desires on a par with your own.

Creating a successful relationship requires both attention and intention. It is based on being secure enough to let your partner know how important they are without losing yourself in the process. It requires you to love and honor your partner and put their needs and desires on a par with your own. Unfortunately, most people don't have the tools to keep reaching out to another once the bloom is off the rose of love. For instance, our natural tendency is to retreat into ourselves when we are faced with an uncomfortable or unfamiliar situation. But it is precisely at this point that you must focus outward if you are to have a fulfilling, intimate relationship.

A first step is to be able to see the world through your partner's eyes. My friend Sandy always spent the same week every year at her parent's beach cottage. Her husband Jack knew how important this week was for Sandy to feel connected to her extended family. Two years ago, Jack won a trip to France during the Tour de France. Sandy was upset because it was at the same time as the yearly beach trip. Jack was an avid cyclist and felt he'd won the jackpot. Sandy ultimately chose to go with Jack because, even though she would rather have not had to deal with the craziness around the race, it was a long-standing dream of Jack's. The longer you are with someone the more your behavior needs to reflect their wants and desires in addition to your own. This is exactly what Sandy did and it made Jack feel loved and important.

Another element necessary to a satisfying relationship is excitement. Excitement releases those important neurotransmitters into your system and reignites that intense initial feeling of connectedness to the relationship. This process recharges the "couple system" and deepens emotional bonds. Stepping outside the normal routine, making time for playfulness and surprise, and focusing on each other on a regular basis can recharge your relationship.

A relationship also requires mutual respect between you and your partner. We often treat complete strangers better than we treat those close to us, but your relationship depends on the consideration you show each other day to day, hour by hour. One way of showing this respect is to let your partner know how important they are to you. It's really easy to take for granted the things your partner does for your relationship on a daily basis. When you take the time to thank your partner for doing the grocery shopping or working hard to provide the vacation opportunities you both like, they feel like what they do matters. While it may be a safe assumption your partner is going to hold down a job or complete a promised chore, acknowledging your partner's effort is important.

It is also important to let your partner see the "real" you. Be honest about your thoughts, feelings, wants, and needs. This is about being vulnerable with, not to, your partner. While being vulnerable can be scary, it can also open the door to greater connection and understanding between you and your partner. By sharing who you are and what you want from life, you are bridging the gap between the two of you and creating something larger and stronger—a truly intimate relationship.

Reveling in the joy of a newfound love is wonderful, but now you understand the constant high it brings is fleeting. Acknowledging the progression of a relationship, and taking conscious steps to work within that progression, will allow you to incorporate this early intensity into a more profound and intimate love that really *can* complete you. Successfully managing this transition will set you and your partner on the road to establishing the foundation for a long and happy marriage.

The creation of your "happily ever after" necessitates a plan, a blueprint if you will. This plan incorporates the wants, needs, hopes, and dreams of both you and your partner. The time and attention you take in developing this blueprint for your life together will determine how well your marriage will stand the test of time. Each stage of this important process is covered in subsequent chapters. This book offers a comprehensive examination of the essential components of a successful marriage, as well as common challenges a marriage can face.

FINAL THOUGHTS

It is important in this day and age of second- and third-generation divorces that couples have the knowledge, tools, and a clear plan to ensure a lasting marriage. While there are some things all marriages have in common, your marriage will, and should, look different from any other marriage. That is because you and your partner are like no one else. You get to decide what part of the tradition that is marriage you want to include in yours, and what you and your partner want to be unique. If you're ready to discover how you can create a blueprint for your marriage, I invite you to read on.

SUGGESTED DESIGN ACTIVITIES

Perhaps now may be a good time to examine your own ideas about the tradition that is marriage and how you might want to make it your own. Finding answers to the following questions, and sharing them with your partner, will help you begin the process of defining what your marriage will look like.

1. What is your idea of what a husband is? A wife?

2. What ideas about marriage did you get from your parents? Your friends?

3. What have you learned from books, movies, or other popular culture about marriage?

4. Is your idea of marriage based on who you want your partner to be, or the living, breathing, wonderful, flawed person you have chosen?

5. What specific behaviors and principles do you want to be present in your marriage?

CHAPTER TWO
BUILDING THE *Us*

The goal in marriage is not to
think alike, but to think together.

– Robert C. Dodds, cleric & counselor

Tom and Maggie were in their mid-20s and had been married about a year when they came to see me. In one of their early sessions, Tom stated: "If I do what Maggie wants, she wins." I had two immediate reactions to this statement. First, didn't Tom want a happy wife? The second thought was a deeper concern: Tom's "you versus me" approach didn't bode well for a successful relationship. Their marriage reflected Tom's point of view, with frequent disagreements over what would be done, when, and how. Issues such as what kind of job Tom should have, what furniture they could afford, and how much time they should spend with Maggie's family all created tension and conflict. Pretty much anything that could be disagreed about was.

In my experience, when people fight about everything, they are really fighting about nothing. These fights are really just an attempt to remain individuals in the face of a perceived effort by their partner to change who they are. I determined that Tom and Maggie were also struggling with the task of defining their relationship in a way that honored their distinct selves but allowed them to develop a workable unit.

BASIS FOR THE *Us*

When I chose to focus my practice on couples work, I quickly learned I would have to find a way to address this very common struggle that Tom and Maggie were experiencing. To guide my work, I searched out information and insights from both professional and popular sources. At one of the first professional conferences I attended, I had the privilege of hearing psychologist Terry Hargrave, Ph.D., give a presentation. He compared a marriage to a couple being in a rowboat on a river, each with only one oar. If the two people row in opposite directions, the boat will remain where it is. If only one person rows at a time, the boat will just turn in a circle. If no one rows, the boat will just drift wherever the current takes it. In order to make any progress, the couple must row together in the same direction and at the same time.

A second source I paid attention to was Phil McGraw, Ph.D. While I know he is somewhat controversial, and I don't always agree with his position, I was struck by his unwavering belief that for a relationship to be successful it takes two "yeses" but only one "no" when it comes to decision-making. This stance struck me as a very healthy way to ensure that neither partner feels pressured into doing something they are not comfortable with.

Willard F. Harley, Jr., Ph.D., a psychotherapist specializing in working with couples, promotes a similar viewpoint in *Marriage Insurance*. He advocates in his "Principle of Joint Agreement" that no action should be taken in a relationship unless both partners are excited about it. While this idea appealed to me on a theoretical level, I struggled with how it would work in practice. Dr. Harley's approach seemed to be relatively easy to implement for decisions couples can foresee, such as where to go on vacation or what type of house to buy. But what about those turning points that come out of the blue? I thought about how Dr. Harley's principle would work if one partner lost their job and had to get another one quickly in order to pay the bills. What if this required moving to another city or state? What if one partner was faced with a life-threatening illness and the couple had different ideas about the course of treatment? I kept struggling with the practical application of this simple concept as I continued through Dr. Harley's book. Finally, about three-quarters of the way through, it hit me: this concept works in all circumstances because that's the way the relationship is set up right from the very beginning. From a small, simple decision to one with potential to alter their lifestyle, a couple who follows this principle will habitually make decisions that honor the relationship, not individual desires.

The idea behind this model is both simple and elegant. Its implementation, on the other hand, is anything but easy. In order for this viewpoint to move from the theoretical into everyday application, it requires a couple to have a mutually agreed-upon life course. While this sounds straightforward, especially when a couple is in the bloom of infatuation, it necessitates a clear under-standing of who each partner is as well as the accompanying expectations of each partner and of the marriage itself.

For example, if one partner grew up watching her parents be physically affectionate, she may view open displays of affection as normal and even expected. As result, she may be hurt or con-fused if her partner rejects her affectionate touching in public. The partners will have to spend some time and energy navigating through this disparity. Negotiating the difficult task of joining two lives with two different perspectives is essential to the long-term success of your relationship. The earlier you begin navigating this potentially bumpy road, the more deliberate and collaborative your relationship will be.

As discussed in the last chapter, couples who want to sustain their bond need to move past infatuation into something deeper and more meaningful. When you are trying to win your partner, you put your best foot forward. Your focus is on the other person. You do things they like to do. You accentuate the areas where you are in agreement and play down, or camouflage, the differences. In other words, you engage in courtship behavior to win your partner's love and hand in marriage. Once the big day is past, you and your partner face the transition to marriage behavior. Your focus needs to shift from the ceremony to the life you want to create. How this transition is managed sets the tone for your entire relationship.

You wonder why your partner seems unwilling to do things your way without realizing you are not willing to do things your partner's way either.

Unfortunately, many people are unaware that they need to make this crucial shift to the *Us*. Instead, once married many people revert back to the "me," returning to the pursuit of their individual goals. Most of us are susceptible to the idea that once we're united, my goals will become your goals and you will meet my needs. This sounds good but here's the problem: your partner is thinking the same thing. All those differences that were put aside when you were dating suddenly move in and fill the room. The differences you didn't talk about before now seem to be the only things you are able to focus on. You wonder why your partner seems unwilling to do things your way without realizing you are not willing to do things your partner's way either. The expectation of "happily ever after" now seems like too much effort for too little return.

In working with my clients, I have discovered that many of their unaddressed issues lie in the perception of courtship behavior being better than marriage behavior. They are honestly shocked by the reality of having to combine two individual paths into a unified vision. At this point, many couples become discouraged—creating a relationship sounds so arduous. Their conclusion reflects the common perception that you have to "work" at marriage. Fortunately, perception is not reality.

In my view, marriage as "work" is an unproductive and disappointing way of looking at one's most intimate partnership. *Marriage requires attention, intention, and commitment, not work.* A strong marriage is formed by the continued focus on meeting your partner's needs and an effort to take their viewpoint into account, without neglecting your own. This involves building on the effort begun during courtship and continuing it at a deeper and more mature level in your marriage.

When you place the attention on your partner, you are more likely to see things from that person's perspective. This opens up possibilities that would be unavailable by staying focused on your own needs and desires. That's not to say that your needs and desires aren't important—they are. But they need to be balanced with those of your partner. Marriage behavior embraces the differences of the couple and combines them in a way that makes the relationship both stronger and more flexible. It is this strength and flexibility that enables marriage to grow and develop over time. This is what makes the difference.

MOVING FORWARD

I experienced this process myself about four years into my own marriage. When we met, my husband was in graduate school working towards his Ph.D. Steve lost about a year of work when his major professor moved from one university to another one across the country. I started work towards a Ph.D. of my own shortly after we married. When he finished his dissertation, we were faced with a dilemma. I still had over a year to go before I could complete mine. Steve had already taken longer than usual to finish and felt he would have a harder time finding a job if he stayed where he was while I finished up. My program would not let me complete my work long distance.

So there we were, two partners faced with incompatible individual goals. Neither of us wanted to hurt the other by proposing that our partner give up their ambition. Steve and I were compelled to examine what we wanted our life together to look like and what path would best get us there. Based on how we saw our life together playing out, realizing our individual potential to maximize our partnership, we decided the wisest course would be to move and allow Steve's career to take priority at this time. I remember telling this story to a co-worker I met just after we moved for my husband's new job. My co-worker, Sam, was appalled that I would "give up my life" and follow my husband like some throwback to the Dark Ages. What Sam didn't understand is that I didn't "give up" anything. I simply made an informed choice to put the health of my relationship ahead of a personal goal that could be fulfilled later. I knew I could always return to school and pursue my chosen career.

The need to balance one's individual goals and the goals of the relationship is an ongoing challenge in all committed relationships. And in truth, no one has been more supportive of my pursuing my current career path than my husband. When I was just starting out as a therapist, my husband was helping me move into my very first office. The doctor I was going to be working with thanked my husband for "letting me work for them." As we were leaving, Steve jokingly said, "When have I ever 'let' you do anything?"

We don't "let" each other do things because this implies we need to ask for our spouse's permission. What we do is remember that *we* asked our spouse to walk through life with us and, therefore, we have an obligation to consider the effect of our actions on their lives. In marriage, the most productive pattern of behavior is to make decisions together that support your collective view of the life you want to build. If you do this for all decisions at all times, you will build a relationship that is a partnership in the truest sense. You will also ensure a fair balance between the needs of the individual and the needs of the marriage.

My husband was able to demonstrate this a few years ago when he accepted a new job. This position required us to move, and that is where the balancing act began. When we visited the town where the company was located, my heart sank. It seemed to me that it was in the middle of nowhere, far from anything that captured my interest or imagination. I was born and raised in Los Angeles and grew up with all sorts of opportunities. I couldn't imagine having any type of life in this small town. A much larger city, with greater options, was just up the highway. Steve understood my disappointment and felt negotiation was reasonable, especially since I had so willingly supported previous moves. He agreed to a 30-minute commute so I could have a more enriched life.

STARTING OUT RIGHT

I believe the best way to transition into marriage is to begin as you intend to go on. This means being clear about what you want your relationship to look like and how you are planning to make that relationship a reality. It requires being able to openly talk to, and negotiate with, your partner over and over again. If you hedge on your own feelings, or count on changing your partner's mind at a later date, you are asking for trouble. This doesn't mean you can't revisit things when circumstances change. But it is much easier to have that conversation if you have already established a history of acknowledging feelings and negotiating needs. The world you set up is the one you are going to have to live in. Make sure it's one that meets the needs of the relationship.

Adam and Theresa came to see me six months after their wedding. Theresa was very upset because she was convinced that Adam no longer loved her. She stated that she was a "horrible wife" and a great disappointment to him. Adam was frustrated because nothing he said or did made any impact on Theresa. Adam stated he felt like he was in a no-win situation. If he complimented Theresa, she would dismiss it as untrue. If he didn't say anything, Theresa would believe he agreed she was a bad wife.

Once I got Theresa to calm down and explain what prompted this sense of panic, it all began to make sense. Theresa's mother sat her down the night before the wedding and explained the "facts of life of marriage." One of those facts was that it was the wife's job to have a hot meal on the table when the husband returned home from a hard day at the office. Theresa was an adequate cook but not a very imaginative one. Theresa also worked in retail and came home after Adam did several nights a week.

In addition, Adam enjoyed good food and, though it wasn't his career, he had learned to cook at one of the best cooking schools in the country. Just recently, Adam had asked Theresa if he could prepare their dinners from now on since he had the time and it was something he really enjoyed doing. Adam truly thought he was making an offer that would help Theresa. When she refused, he had been hurt and confused. He had no idea he was triggering Theresa's unconscious fear of being an inadequate partner.

Adam knew how Theresa's mother was about things being "just right." What he didn't know was how much Theresa had adopted her mother's viewpoint. While they were dating, everything had seemed balanced and equal between them. Whenever something needed to be done, whichever one of them was available did it. There had never been any discussion of a man's job versus a woman's. Adam was completely dumbfounded when he finally understood what had upset Theresa. As they talked more about what each had learned growing up and their unspoken expectations of themselves and their partner in a marriage, Adam and Theresa were able to sort through how they each wanted to be in the marriage. More importantly, they were able to let go of expectations that didn't support their vision.

CONCESSIONS VS. ACCOMMODATIONS

It is my experience that many couples, like Adam and Theresa, start doing things in their relationship because they think they're supposed to, regardless of whether it makes sense for them. Once started, this pattern becomes very difficult to change. The transition into marriage is the time to establish the rules, boundaries, and traditions a couple wishes to live by. Unfortunately, it is also during this time that many unspoken assumptions are made. It is essential that both partners be clear about their expectations of their partner as well as what each is willing to do.

For example, if you don't mind doing laundry then by all means go ahead. If, however, it is a chore you detest, don't take it on in the hope that one day your partner will have an epiphany about your true feelings and rescue you from a lifetime of self-imposed drudgery. It's much more likely that your partner won't realize you are being a martyr. Don't assume that your partner can read your mind. Instead, speak up about your needs and preferences. Don't let resentment build.

When silent resentment is allowed to grow, it is like a cancer that can choke the life from your relationship. Resentment often starts with a concession. I define a concession as agreeing to do something you don't want to do. Two things can happen when you do this. First, if you agree to do something and then don't follow through, your partner is likely to feel betrayed and hurt because you broke a promise. If this happens too frequently, your partner will become resentful over what they interpret to be your lies. The second option is that you dutifully do what you said you would do even though you don't want to. However, you do it with clenched fists and a tight jaw, because you are filled with resentment.

Clearly, neither outcome is healthy for the relationship. This resentment one partner feels often lies just below the surface, seething and roiling. It may take years to come out but, make no mistake, it will come out. People make concessions all the time for varying reasons. Sometimes they want to avoid a difficult conversation. Sometimes they say whatever they think they need to say to stop an argument. Sometimes, like Theresa, they think it's something they *should* do. Whatever the reason, making a concession is always a mistake. Why? Because it breeds resentment that leeches like poison into the relationship and churns below the surface. It may take years to erupt, but it will eventually blow. These eruptions take many forms: withdrawing from conversations or activities, refusing to fulfill responsibilities, having an affair, and, ultimately, filing for divorce.

The flip side to doing what you think is expected—even when you don't want to—is not doing the things you *should*. This is equally detrimental to the relationship. Remember my client Tom who told me he shouldn't have to do what his wife wanted because then she would win? This common perspective sets up the relationship as a competition and lays the groundwork for keeping score. By definition, if one person is winning the other person must be losing. This pattern results in one-upmanship, hurt feelings, and anger. If the patterns continue uninterrupted, one or both partners may refuse to meet the other's needs, withhold affection, and/or use sexual intimacy as a weapon. The result is an unhealthy and unhappy relationship that becomes vulnerable to those needs getting met from the outside, such as by an affair.

So what, you ask, should partners do instead? The best choice is to make an accommodation. By this I mean that you agree to do only those things you genuinely consent to do. It may not be a choice you ever would have considered, left to your own devices. But it is something that you are willing to look at from all angles and decide you can live with without resentment.

Sometimes the choice falls in line with what one of you wants to do. Sometimes it is a negotiated solution that falls somewhere between both of your ideals. Your decision may not come about immediately but you and your partner are willing to stay with it until you find a solution you both can accept and honor without harboring ill feelings. When you and your partner make *intentional accommodations*, not *reactive concessions*, you are successfully navigating the ebb and flow that characterizes all long-term relationships.

CREATING AN *US*

One of the most difficult tasks you face as a newly married couple is the joining of your two separate lives into one connected one. If this undertaking is not effectively completed, the marriage will not be as happy or successful as it could be. The joy you experienced on your wedding day will slowly fade over time unless this feeling is carefully, and consciously, nurtured.

But contrary to popular opinion, this process of nurture doesn't need to be "work." I believe if a couple manages the primary mission of melding two lives into one with skill and deliberation, the foundation of the relationship will be solid enough that work is not necessary. This does not mean the couple won't have to continue to pay attention to the relationship and act with the intention of preserving it. It does mean this should be an issue of thoughtful maintenance, not challenging construction.

By marrying, two individuals are asking each other to walk through life side by side. This is a wonderful and romantic idea. Putting this idea into practice is another thing entirely. All at once, each person is no longer responsible solely for themselves. Each action taken by one partner affects the other. For individuals accustomed to doing what they want, when they want, and how they want, suddenly having to take another person's needs and desires into account can be quite disruptive. How you as a couple address this challenge sets the tone for the relationship.

I believe that a happy and successful marriage must be built on the concept of the *Us*. The *Us* is a third entity that is created from the needs and wants of each member of the couple. It is the goals, dreams, and plans that the couple negotiates for their life together. This *Us* has its own personality, likes, dislikes, and preferred activities. The concept of this third influence in a marriage was introduced and explored by Dr. Terry Hargrave in his book, *The Essential Humility of Marriage*. It is also the driving force behind the relationship. Every decision either member of the couple makes is considered in terms of the *Us*. If the outcome moves the couple towards its goals then the action is taken. If the outcome is not in the best interest of the couple, then—no matter how much one party wants to do it—the action is not taken. The *Us* is like an umbrella that both protects the couple and serves to connect the two individuals.

The concept of the *Us* can be misunderstood as one of subservience to your partner. This is definitely not what I mean. You each remain who you are. It is very important not to lose one's individual self to a relationship. When you and your partner create an *Us*, you are merely putting the needs of the couple ahead of your own individual wants and desires. Note, I did not say ahead of each partner's individual needs. The needs of each individual are included in the definition of the *Us*. It is their wants and desires that are negotiated as part of the *Us*. If one partner's wants conflict with what the couple has defined as their *Us*, that individual either abandons the desired action or the couple renegotiates the *Us* to accommodate it.

THE PURPOSE OF EMOTIONAL NEEDS

In discussions of the elements of marital success, the role that emotional needs play in a committed relationship often goes unaddressed. Abraham Maslow introduced the concept of "belonging needs" as the third level in his hierarchy of needs theory. The first two levels deal with our physical survival needs, such as the need for food and the need to be protected from the elements. When these needs are taken care of, our focus turns to our need for friends, a sweetheart, and for being part of a community. It is this set of emotional needs that drives our desire to belong to the "in" crowd, the sports team, and even our desire for marriage and a family. If this emotional need to belong is not met, we become susceptible to loneliness and social anxiety. According to Maslow, this type of need is considered a "deficit need." By this, he means that if the need is not met in an adequate way, you will *feel* the need for it. If, however, you get all you need of this sense of belonging, you will be content.

This concept of belonging needs, also referred to as "emotional needs" by Dr. Harley in *His Needs, Her Needs*, becomes very important in terms of the success of your relationship. If one of your emotional needs is not met in your relationship, you will feel a deficit. Because it is a need, not a want, you will try to get that need met any way you can. If it is not met within your primary relationship, you may try to meet it outside your relationship. This is why it is absolutely necessary that your and your partner's emotional needs are part of the *Us* you create.

Often, the genuine needs of your partner are dismissed as just something your partner "wants" and as something that may or may not be important to you. This happens because you, or your partner, have not identified what those needs are and how they need to play out in your relationship. One way of looking at these needs is to examine how you or your partner feel connected to others. Do you connect by physical touch, conversation, engaging in an activity together, or by having certain actions acknowledged? These behaviors correspond to basic needs such as affection, communication, recreational participation, and admiration.

One way to identify whether something is a need or a want is to imagine never having it again in your life. If never getting a hug or hearing a compliment again makes you apprehensive or anxious, it is probably one of your needs. While it is true that your first priority is to get your physical needs met, having your emotional needs met is almost as important. Human beings are communal creatures. We are part of families, clans, and tribes. We need each other to survive. Your belonging or emotional needs are what keep you connected to the people in your life. They are also important for a feeling of overall health and well-being. The key is in knowing what your needs are and getting them met in a healthy and productive way. This is an essential step in defining your *Us*. Being able to get your needs met, and meeting the needs of your partner, are essential to a strong, happy, and protected marriage.

WHAT ARE SOME OF YOUR EMOTIONAL NEEDS?

In talking with my clients about their emotional needs, I often find confusion about what exactly qualifies. So let's look at what might qualify as a genuine need. The following list, adapted from *His Needs, Her Needs* by Willard Harley, Ph.D., is not meant to be exhaustive, but rather a way to stimulate your thinking.

ADMIRATION: A deep desire to be respected and valued. It is having your accomplishments and hard work acknowledged on a regular basis. Getting satisfaction from receiving praise, getting awards, or otherwise being noticed by others in a positive way would be an indication that you have this need.

AFFECTION: A deep desire to feel important to another and to be cared for by them. It can be a physical act such as a hug, a tangible gift such as a note or flowers, or a loving action such as a back rub or a kind word. Enjoying being touched in a nonsexual way, being in romantic situations, or receiving compliments would indicate this need is important to you.

APPRECIATION: A deep desire to have your actions acknowledged by others. It is receiving thanks for the efforts you make on behalf of that person. It is recognition of the time and energy you invest in making another person's life slightly better or easier. Feeling taken for granted or unimportant when you do things for others is an indication of this need.

ATTRACTIVENESS: A deep desire to be around attractive people. It is noticing what others look like and how they behave, sometimes to the point of being distracted from what you're supposed to be doing. If it's important to you that your partner takes the time to look their best or acts in a way that brings an admiring glance from others, this need may be important for you.

CONVERSATION: A deep desire to verbally share thoughts, feelings, hopes, and dreams with another person. It involves the desire to gather information about another person, such as their likes, interests, and views on life. Getting energy from verbally interacting with others is an indication of this need.

FINANCIAL SAFETY: A deep desire to be financially secure. It involves a clear understanding of what is expected of both you and your partner regarding how income is earned and how money is managed. If issues surrounding money or financial stability make you anxious, this need is probably important to you.

OPENNESS: A deep desire for your partner to share their private thoughts and feelings freely with you. It involves a sense of being thought trustworthy enough to gently hold your partner's vulnerabilities with love and great care. Wanting to know what others are thinking and feeling without having to probe and/or feeling you can hold others' cares and concerns with honor are indications of this need.

ORDER: A deep desire to have a peaceful and well-managed living environment. It involves a sense of organization, tidiness, and predictability that allows you to function in an anxiety-free manner. Finding yourself frazzled or uncomfortable if your surroundings are cluttered is an indication you might have this need. Being able to predict your partner's responses and actions both in a given situation and over time are part of this need as well.

RECREATIONAL PARTICIPATION: A deep desire to engage in enjoyable activities with another person. These activities can range from doing something athletic to attending cultural events to shopping. Traveling and sharing new experiences may also be part of this need. Actively engaging in recreational pursuits with another person indicates importance of this need.

SEXUAL SATISFACTION: A deep desire to be physically and sexually intimate with another person. This desire may be expressed by wanting to make love to your current partner but is present even when you are not in a relationship. Having strong and frequent sexual fantasies and/or an active sex life might indicate this need.

THE IMPACT OF EMOTIONAL NEEDS

Don and Peggy were in dire straits when they came to my office. They were a handsome couple in their late thirties with three children. Their problems intensified after the birth of their youngest daughter, Emily, six years earlier. It was a difficult birth because the baby was breech and had the cord wrapped around her neck. Emily had to be kept in the intensive care unit for three weeks.

As a result, she had been sleeping with Don and Peggy since she came home from the hospital. Every time Don suggested that Emily move to her own room, Peggy would become hysterical and accuse Don of not caring about their daughter's health. She was convinced Emily would stop breathing in the night. Peggy had grown cold and distant toward Don over the years because she was angry that he didn't appreciate her devotion to their daughter. Their physical intimacy had dwindled over these years until it was nearly nonexistent.

Don was desperate to save his 15-year marriage. "I'll do anything to get things back on track with Peggy," he told me in our first session. Peggy was equally adamant that she was just being a good mother and Don should just "get over it." "Don is just a selfish man who is only interested in sex. It would be perfectly fine with me if we never have sex again. I'm very upset that Don just takes all the things I do for him and the kids for granted," Peggy added.

The yawning chasm in their marriage was reflected by the physical distance Peggy put between them in my office. Every time Don would try to sit next to her, or reach out to take her hand, Peggy would pull further into her corner of the sofa as if the mere contact with him would leave her physically burned. The day she said she felt assaulted when he hugged her I saw the pain and hopelessness in Don's eyes. Don declared to Peggy, "I'll give up ever having sex again if you will just let me hold your hand." I knew at that moment he had no understanding of what he was suggesting.

Don's yearning to be physically intimate with Peggy was an emotional need he could not deny. The same was true of Peggy's need to be appreciated and admired for the sacrifices she made for her family. I explained to them that asking each other to live without getting their fundamental needs met was neither realistic nor productive. Once each understood the other wasn't being unreasonable or selfish, they were able to stop fighting and really start understanding what the other needed. Don began to pay attention to all the effort Peggy put into caring for the family. He made a point to acknowledge this effort daily. Peggy began to relax more around Don and stopped perceiving every attempt at physical contact as a come-on for sex.

Understanding and meeting your partner's emotional needs, and having yours met in return, ensures you both will feel safe and secure in the relationship. In addition, recognizing your partner's requests as a means of getting their needs met and becoming more connected to you can change how you respond to those requests. If you can adopt the viewpoint that this is something your partner cannot control, instead of something your partner is doing just to annoy you, you are more likely to feel compassionate and understanding. Your partner, in turn, may find you more approachable and open—and may also begin to be more open to *your* needs. This change in behavior will allow you both to have the capacity and foundation to negotiate a productive and supportive *Us*.

FINAL THOUGHTS: A WIN-WIN PERSPECTIVE

It is important to remember that the *Us* is not a static arrangement. It is a living, breathing entity that changes and grows as the couple that constructed it changes and grows. The sole purpose of the *Us* is to provide a framework for both your day-to-day actions and for the long-term structure of your relationship. Its presence ensures that the health of your relationship is as important as the mental and emotional health of you and your partner. Creation of the *Us* elevates the idea of the couple as equal to that of each individual. This eliminates Tom's idea that if Maggie wins, he, by default, loses. Neither you nor your partner wins or loses if an *Us* is the foundation of your relationship. Instead, you, as a couple, win every time.

SUGGESTED DESIGN ACTIVITIES

The following are some questions that will help you and your partner define and create your *Us*. You each should take your time and answer as fully and carefully as you can. Once both of you have identified your positions, find an appropriate time and place to discuss them fully with each other. Remember, your goal is to work together to design your happily-ever-after.

1. Clearly define what you want your marriage to look like.

2. What concessions have you made in your past relationships? Your current one?

3. Identify where you could have made accommodations.

4. What are your emotional needs? Your partner's?

5. Define the underlying guidelines of your *Us*.

CHAPTER 3

FOUNDATION OF THE *Us*: KNOW WHO YOU ARE

What counts in making a happy marriage
is not how compatible you are,
but how you handle the incompatibility.

– Leo Tolstoy, author

One question I am often asked is, "How do I know if the person I'm with is the 'right one'?" From fairy tales, romantic movies, and even our friends and family, we are bombarded with the fantasy of finding our one true soulmate. It is drilled into us that unless we find our other half, we are doomed to lead unfulfilled and unhappy lives. Think about one of the most frequently quoted, and (completely misguided) romantic lines of popular culture: "You complete me," from the movie *Jerry McGuire*. It implies that we need another person to be fulfilled.

In fact, quite the opposite is true. You don't need a relationship with another person to "complete" you. You need to be whole in yourself before you can join with another to form a healthy relationship.

LESSONS FROM A FAIRY TALE

From the time she was a little girl, Monica dreamed of her wedding day. She had watched all the Disney movies and concluded there was no reason why she, too, couldn't grow up to be a princess. All she had to do was find her Prince Charming.

Once Monica started college, she began her prince search in earnest. The tradition at the women-only college she attended was to get the school ring junior year and a diamond ring as a senior. Monica met Tom halfway through her junior year at a Christmas formal her sorority held with his fraternity from a nearby university. He was fairly attractive, athletic, and came from a good family. He was majoring in economics and had a job waiting for him in the family business. Tom "surprised" Monica with the coveted diamond engagement ring on New Year's Eve of her senior year. Tom was an acceptable catch and, if he didn't match all of a prince's characteristics, Monica was pretty sure that she could whip him into shape. Five years and one baby later Monica and Tom were in my office trying to figure out what had gone wrong.

Monica had concentrated on the wrong part of the fairy tales. She had focused on the happy ending of the stories and forgotten about how those endings had come about. All of the great love stories have one thing in common: the two lovers have to struggle to be together. Whether it is an outside force, like a wicked witch or social expectations, or some life circumstance, such as being attracted to someone from a very different background, obstacles are placed in the path of true love. In these stories, it is only when partners reach inside themselves and find ways to overcome these complications that the characters find their way back to each other and create their "happily ever after."

When you look closely at these stories, you see that the factors that allow for success come from realizations each individual has about *what's really important to them*. These revelations require thoughtful analysis about oneself that is triggered by the challenges the characters face. It's not that lasting love must involve suffering, but it does require clear, tough-minded self-knowledge. Unfortunately, Monica chose Tom not because she determined that he was a truly good match for her, but because he was a "suitable enough" and fit into her time frame for marriage. She was working with the wrong criteria.

THE FOUNDATION OF YOUR RELATIONSHIP

The strength of a relationship, like the strength of a house, is its foundation. If a house's foundation is not properly laid, the house will sag, shift, and eventually collapse. Therefore, great care must be taken to build a solid foundation. Most foundations are made of concrete, which is basically a mixture of rock and water. How these two ingredients are combined—the proportion of each present and the thorough mixing of them—will determine the strength and durability of the house.

> **Before you can join with another,
> you have to know who you are
> and what you need.**

So it is with your relationship. The amount of each person that is added to the mixture and how completely the two people combine themselves will predict the power and intensity of the partnership. In order to know what each person can bring to the *Us*, it is absolutely essential to complete the first step in the process. Before you can join with another, you have to know who you are and what you need. Everyone has a core self that defines them and guides their behavior. This core must be identified and included in the *Us*. If any part of this core is left out, the foundation of the relationship is automatically weakened. You cannot afford to negotiate away anything that you consider part of your core self.

This process of defining who you are and what you need should be approached with great care and intent. It is the basis for the relationship, and therefore the life, you will create. There are three major elements of this process that must be clearly defined if you are to successfully form a strong foundation.

FINDING THE YOU. Your core consists of the unique qualities that make you who you are. It is made up of your morals, your values, your temperament, and the experiences that have shaped you. No one's core is quite like another's. For example, most of us would say that honesty and integrity are part of our core. What makes these qualities distinctive for a particular person is how they are applied. For instance, one person might hold a strict view of honesty that does not allow for even the accidental removal of a paper clip, while their partner might be quite comfortable telling little white lies that spare the feelings of others. Both of these individuals may value honesty and integrity, but have differing levels of tolerance for deviating from the ideal. They may, however, be able to negotiate their relationship so it is based on complete honesty except in those instances when someone's feelings would get hurt. You want to identify those things that make you the person you are. You also need to be clear about where you are willing to bend and negotiate. This allows you to define and maintain the boundaries that will prevent you from losing yourself in the relationship.

WHAT YOU WANT IN A MATE. Over the course of your dating life you probably had experiences that helped you clarify the qualities you wanted in your life partner. You may have started out with vague generalities (someone close to your age or with a similar lifestyle) or you may have had a daunting list of "must haves" (certain height, weight, hair color, figure type, salary, etc.). As you dated, entered into longer relationships, and left them, your qualifications for the person you were willing to invest substantial time and energy in probably became somewhat clearer. You continued to refine these qualifications to the ones that were absolutely essential and then eliminated from serious consideration anyone who did not meet them. You eventually found that special some-one and entered into a lifelong commitment with them.

ENVISION YOUR RELATIONSHIP. In addition to identifying what you need from a mate, it is also vital to identify what you need from a relationship. The relationship is where you intend to get your emotional needs met. Your partner is the one you want to help you meet them. Many people believe these are one and the same. It would be a mistake to think that.

By this I mean that what you want your relationship to look like is separate from the personalities and the experiences of the two people in that relationship. It is essential that you know what components need to be present in this primary relationship (your emotional needs) and clearly define what having those needs met entails. While your chosen partner does have to be compat-ible with you in many ways, they do not have to have an identical vision. The two of you must be willing to negotiate your needs into a common vision you both can support.

For example, some of us grew up in homes where feelings were openly expressed either with words or actions. If you know that you need emotion expressed by physical contact with another, such as a kiss goodbye or holding hands at the movies, you need to ensure your partner is comfortable with that. If you need to hear the words "I love you" spoken on a regular basis, those words should flow relatively freely from your partner. This may be some-thing your partner might have to learn to be comfortable with. Very early in our relationship, my husband told me not to expect to hear those words very often. I thought about it and decided that since actions are more important to me than words, I was okay with that. Much to our mutual surprise, my husband now says those words to me almost every day. While I don't recommend that you pin your hopes on that kind of change occurring in your relationship, when it happens, it's a bonus!

WHAT OUR PAST TEACHES US

When Cathy came to my office for help, she was in her late twenties. By then, she had been involved with Lewis for three years. They were living together and talking seriously about getting married. Cathy was seeking guidance on whether she should ignore her feelings of discontent in order to fulfill her dream of being part of a committed couple. Cathy had been down this path before. She would meet a guy and immediately start planning their future together. She became single-mindedly interested in whatever he mentioned. The restaurant he wanted to go to, the movie he wanted to see, or the activity he wanted to do, Cathy was always ready and willing. Her mother had taught her that this was the way to land a husband.

This pattern of putting her partner's desires first had continued with Lewis. In addition, Cathy put up with Lewis being a slob. He would never pick up after himself and the thought of actually cleaning their apartment never entered his mind. Cathy had done all the straightening and cleaning since they moved in together. She believed it was her job as the woman. However, Cathy wanted to buy a house but wasn't sure she wanted to take on the responsibility for more space when she could barely keep up with the small apartment.

In the middle of a particularly emotional therapy session, Cathy revealed that since high school, the longest time she'd ever been without a boyfriend was three months. She also admitted she had never been the one to do the breaking up. Almost as soon as one relationship ended, Cathy looked for another one. Slumped down into the chair, she seemed at a complete loss to understand why her relationships always seemed to follow the same pattern.

Cathy thought she was giving her partners exactly what they wanted, but the relationships all ended up in a series of arguments and recriminations. "When I would mention my frustration over not having time to do something I wanted to do and ask for some help, the fights would start," Cathy stated. "My partner would expect me to do something I did all the time but I would get really upset this time and let him have it." Sometimes her partner would make an attempt to give Cathy what she wanted in hopes of calming her down, but the change would never last more than a couple of weeks and things would return to the same old, same old. Eventually both of them would get so tired and frustrated with the discord, the relationship would end. Cathy was seeing the beginnings of this pattern with Lewis and wanted to find a way out of it.

She had an "aha" moment one day when I asked her why what Lewis wanted was more important than what she wanted. I could almost see the light bulb go off over her head when she said out loud, "I'm afraid Lewis will leave me if I don't do what he wants."

Cathy finally "got it." She recognized she wanted to be in a relationship so badly that she was willing to do almost anything, including discounting her own needs. When Cathy could no longer ignore her needs and requested they be met, the problems would start. She also discovered that she minimized the way Lewis made her feel, hoping he would change those behaviors after marriage. When Cathy realized the pattern of her relationships was driven by her fear of being alone, she made the decision to put off marriage until she and Lewis had developed a more equal relationship.

Cathy, like many of us, didn't make the connection between her fear of being alone and her failed relationships. She thought that if she could just give her partner everything he wanted and require little in return, the relationship would work out. The problem with this way of thinking is that it ignores a basic reality about relationships: it's an interaction between two people. When that relationship addresses the needs of only one of the parties, it results in an imbalance that cannot be sustained over the long run.

If either party is motivated by fear of losing that relationship, the other party will then have a disproportionate influence, even if they are unaware of it. A pattern of one person giving in to the needs of the other will develop. Concessions accumulate. The person on the "getting" end becomes comfortably happy with this pattern, and becomes highly resistant to change. Conflict becomes inevitable. If you don't require that your needs be met right from the beginning, developing the type of relationship that sustains you will require the work most people associate with marriage.

THE PRICE OF FEAR

When Samantha first came to see me she was upset about her difficult relationship with her daughter and her ex-husband. She extolled the virtues of her current significant other, Ron. "He is incredibly supportive and understanding," she told me. In subsequent sessions, however, Samantha revealed details about her relationship that made me question her Pollyanna view of things.

"I'm sorry for being late. I had to wait for Ron to come home," Samantha said. "Even though the car is mine, he insists on driving me everywhere." She also said that the money used to purchase their condominium was from her divorce settlement; the condo was in Ron's name. "I don't understand," she stated. "Ron gets upset with me if I want to do something other than what he wants, but then he calls me 'overly sensitive' or 'irrational' if I get upset with him."

At our last session, Samantha told me she cancelled a doctor's appointment it took her three months to get because Ron wanted her to go with him to walk the dog and she wouldn't get back in time to make the appointment. When I asked her why she would do that, and why he would let her, Samantha looked confused. She stated, "I'm supposed to do whatever it takes to make the relationship work." She seemed to accept completely that Ron's view of how things should be was correct and she was "wrong" if she wanted something different. It never occurred to Samantha that her view of how the relationship should be was just as "right" as Ron's.

Samantha's lack of appropriate boundaries limited her ability to require her partner to treat her with dignity and respect. As a result, she was always willing to adjust her schedule, activities, and thoughts to match those of whoever she was with at the time. (This pattern of not standing up for herself also affected her relationship with her daughter. She believed her daughter wouldn't like her if Samantha enforced any limitations on her behavior.) The more she allowed it to happen, the more she believed everyone else was right about what she should do and that she was wrong.

Not surprisingly, this pattern affected Samantha's ability to trust her own judgments and feelings. Once her belief in her own capabilities was compromised, so was her self-esteem. It became a vicious cycle: the lower her self-esteem, the more she depended on the views of others and less on herself, which resulted in even lower self-esteem. The end result was an even lower opinion of her by her partner and the continued deterioration of the relationship. I worked with Samantha on identifying what is opinion and what is fact. She then applied this process to evaluating her opinion against that of her partner. Samantha eventually learned to judge her decisions on what was right for her, instead of automatically altering her behavior to match someone else's opinion. Much to her surprise, but not mine, Ron began to accept her decisions and the relationship became more equitable.

NOT RIGHT OR WRONG, JUST DIFFERENT

Like Samantha, many of us accept our partner's position as fact and not the opinion it actually is. Instead of recognizing a difference in equally valid viewpoints, we believe our partner when they say they are right. The problem with this is that if one person is always wrong, the power balance of the relationship is tipped in the other's favor. The "wrong" partner will spend considerable time and energy trying to make it up to the "right" partner but will never be successful.

The premise of "right" and "wrong" must be summarily rejected at the outset. Your perceptions, feelings, and needs are not right or wrong. They just are. It shouldn't become a contest if your partner has different feelings and needs. One sign of a healthy relationship is the ability of partners to accept the differences in perception or viewpoint and not feel compelled to eliminate them. It is always acceptable to explain your feelings and opinions to your partner. You should never have to defend them.

If you don't feel able to freely express your own feelings and needs, you will begin to resent your partner's manipulations and believe they are trying to control you. You may make an effort from time to time to put forth your perspective or desires, but your fear stops you from really pressing the issue. What you have done is make a concession to your partner. You have also allowed the seeds of resentment to take hold in your relationship. Those seeds may take many years to flower, but if you can identify and then eliminate them, you can protect your relationship.

HONORING THE *US*

Creating a mutually respectful *Us* involves learning how to make accommodations in your relationship, not concessions. As described earlier, accommodations are decisions made from a well-thought-out position, not a fear-based one. In an accommodation, all possibilities are put on the table and examined for how they will impact the *Us*. Any decisions made are in accordance with the goals and values of the *Us*. Each partner allows the other to express any feelings, concerns, or opinions about a particular option without judgment or pressure. The partners keep working through these options until consensus is reached. A balance between the desire of the individuals and the needs of the *Us* must be maintained if resentment is to be avoided and the relationship protected.

Don and Angie had been married for two years when Don was offered the job of his dreams. It would require moving across the country and closer to his family, people Angie didn't really know. Angie had lived her whole life in Iowa, where most of her family still lived, and had never considered living in the Pacific Northwest. She really loved the farmland and friendly people she grew up with in her home town. In addition, she had just found out she was pregnant and was really counting on her mother and sisters to help her once the baby was born.

Angie was quite upset for a few weeks as she tried to get her head around the drastic change Don wanted them to make. She knew this job would allow them the financial freedom for her to stay at home with the baby. She also was able to see it as an opportunity to get to know her mother-in-law better. Once she and Don visited the city where they would live and she saw all the green trees and beautiful wildflowers that lined the highways, Angie was able to imagine the life they could build. She began to see how it might work out and was able to face the possible move with acceptance.

Angie was able to make this decision only because she was aware of who she was and what was important to her. She and Don were able to calmly discuss options because each put the needs of the relationship first. They didn't come by this process accidentally. It came out of mutual respect, common goals, and the ability to maintain their own sense of identity while still being part of something bigger.

PROTECTING YOUR NEEDS

When our partner doesn't meet our needs, it is easy to conclude that they "don't care" about us. But sometimes the problem is simply that we haven't taken the steps necessary to ensure that our needs will be met. Once you've identified your emotional needs, it is *your* job to get them met.

This doesn't mean you need to become demanding or difficult. It does mean you need to be persistent. Your partner may not be meeting your need because you have been too vague or unclear in your requests for them to know what you want. Many times, however, your partner may resist your request because it makes them uncomfortable. Change is often uncomfortable—even healthy change. So your partner may choose to believe your request isn't that important to you or that you won't really mind if your appeal is unmet.

It isn't that your partner doesn't love you or doesn't want you to be happy. They are just hoping it doesn't have to be at the expense of having to change their behavior. If you let your request for getting a need met drop, your partner is likely to conclude that you are okay with the status quo and go on believing that everything is fine between you. I can't emphasize this enough. *If you let your need drop, the assumption is that you agree.* The problem, of course, is that you don't agree. The more your needs get squashed, the more your resentment will build.

Gary and Suzanne had been married ten years and had a four-year-old daughter when they came to my office. For most of the marriage, Gary had been unhappy with the frequency of their sex life. He would bring it up with Suzanne on occasion. Sometimes there would be improvement for a while, sometimes not. Gary loved Suzanne and the two of them got along very well—except for this one area. Most of the time, he would push his dissatisfaction into the background because everything else was so good.

We talked about each one's view of sex in a marriage and any unresolved resentments. "I know it is important to Gary and I don't think he's being unreasonable. It's just that since the baby was born, I just don't seem to have the desire," Suzanne explained. "I'm not an oaf and I take care of myself," Gary said. "I just don't know what else to do." Suzanne heard the frustration and hurt in Gary's voice and things got better until Suzanne went back to work. Caring for a young child and working full-time took a lot of her energy. Even though Gary helped a lot with the household chores, intimate relations between them returned to the old pattern.

The final straw was on Gary's birthday. After having a romantic dinner and a wonderful night out, Suzanne rejected Gary's advances once again. Gary shut down and turned away for good from Suzanne. Once this happened, Suzanne finally understood Gary's need for physical intimacy was a need, not just a wish or a preference. But it was too late. Even though they still loved each other, the relationship had taken one hit too many. By the time they returned to my office, Gary was seriously thinking about divorce.

Gary had tried over the years to get Suzanne to understand how important physical intimacy was to him. The problem was Gary was neither consistent nor persistent enough in requiring his need be met. He allowed Suzanne's discomfort in this area to override his responsibility to get his need met. Every time Gary conceded to Suzanne's position, he could see her anxiety lessen, which made him feel that backing off was the "right" thing to do. Gary often felt that if he pushed the issue he would be perceived as an uncaring lout.

You have to take ownership of your needs and work with your partner to get them met. Getting the need met is not negotiable, but *how* the need gets met is. You and your partner must find mutually agreeable solutions to getting both of your needs met. It is part of the process of developing your *Us*. Both of you need to be willing to teach and learn about your respective needs so that your individual emotional needs can become the emotional needs of the *Us*.

Because this process of negotiating the *Us* may be a new concept for you and your partner, you will need to be patient as you help each other through the anxiety or discomfort that may be present. It is a process that will take some time. With love and perseverance you and your partner will be successful. Meeting each other's needs is a skill that can—and must—be learned if you want to develop and maintain a healthy, happy relationship based on love and respect.

Final Thoughts

If you are willing to embrace the important concept of the *Us* as it relates to the success of your marriage, you must be willing to start at the beginning. Understanding who you are and what's important to you is an essential undertaking if you are to have any hope of finding a compatible partner. The next step is to identify the traits and characteristics your model partner ought to have. Ideally, this person will be both compatible with and complementary to you. Once you and this person have found each other, you can then set about building your life together. You and your partner have identified your individual needs and have set about combining them into the needs of your *Us*. Finally, you and your partner are ready to take the next step.

Suggested Design Activities

The following are activities meant to help you define what is important to you and how that fits with what you want your marriage to look like. Once you have a clear vision, you and your partner can refine what you are currently doing to make that vision a reality.

1. Define who you are as a person and what is important to you.

2. Make a list of traits and characteristics you found compatible in your partner.

3. Write a job description for the ideal spouse.

4. Identify what you need from a relationship.

5. Identify actions you need to take to ensure your emotional needs are met by your partner.

CHAPTER 4
WALLS OF THE *Us:*
HONOR YOUR COMMITMENT

Happy marriages begin when we marry the ones we love,
and blossom when we love the ones we marry.

– Tom Mullen, author

On the day of your wedding, you and your partner stood before friends and family, taking part in a ceremony that may have been more than a year in the making. You promised to love, honor, and cherish each other, forsaking all others until death parts you. The gathered company in turn promised to support you in keeping these vows.

But what exactly is everyone committing to do? What will keep you and your partner from dissolving this very public commitment a few years later as many others do? How can your friends and family honor the commitment they made that long-ago day to support your marriage as the two of you navigate life's ups and downs?

Your wedding day is a time when you and your partner look forward to your future life with great anticipation and excitement. It may, however, also be a time to recognize the most important challenge of this future—the challenge to join two individual lives into a strong, united couple. The vows you took to love, honor, and cherish each other can be a roadmap to that happy future of your dreams. Making a conscious choice to put these vows into practice on a daily basis will go far in helping you to make that transition to a successful union. You can walk the path to a long, happy marriage by intentionally creating your *Us*. Part of this process involves clearly defining what your vows mean and actively honoring those vows in your relationship. It is vital that you and your partner understand what you meant when you vowed to love, honor, and cherish each other.

LOVE

Loving your partner means protecting them from harm. This includes harm from outside of the relationship (people or situations that cause stress) as well as inside it (your own anger, resentment, etc.). Love is about making sure your partner feels safe and secure in the relationship. This means you must have your partner's back in all things and at all times. If you find yourself in a public situation where you must choose to either support your partner or side with someone else, you pick your partner every time. This steadfast support allows your partner to feel like a priority to you.

Loving your partner means protecting them from harm.

It's not a question of agreeing with your partner in every situation—that's not realistic. But to the outside world you need to be seen as a united team. You keep your disagreements private so your partner never feels abandoned or alone. The same goes for publicly correcting your partner's speech or behavior. If your partner makes an error that you think could cause them some embarrassment or other harm, ask your partner if they would like your help fixing it. If you wouldn't publicly correct a stranger, don't do it to your partner.

Love also means you never intentionally hurt your partner by punishing them, making judgments, using demeaning words or a harsh tone, or using anger as a weapon. When someone loves you it gives you the power to hurt. So when you disagree, you must do so with respect and kindness. You know where your partner is vulnerable, and when you promised to love them it meant that you would never use your partner's weaknesses against them. It is never necessary—and always harmful—to lay waste to your partner out of anger or a sense of righteousness. Your tone, body language, and choice of words have the power to do deep and lasting damage to your relationship.

It is also unloving to diminish your partner's feelings. You may not feel the same way your partner does in a particular situation, but your partner is neither stupid nor overly sensitive for feeling the way they do. Becoming aware of and honoring your partner's emotional needs is vital. Ignoring those feelings and sensitivities tells your partner you don't care about them. Instead, you can express your love for your partner by providing a safe place to freely share their deepest feelings.

Loving your partner also means modifying any behavior that is annoying or hurtful. If your partner makes a reasonable request about changing a habit, it is an act of love on your part to try to honor that request, even if it isn't that important to you or you don't fully understand why your partner wants it. The important thing is that you have the ability to make your partner happy. If you can, you should.

Early on in my marriage, I was a manager in a department store. As soon as I got home each evening, I would take off my shoes and leave them wherever they landed. Since I had many pairs of shoes, this added up to a lot of kicked-off footwear. My husband made several requests that I not leave my shoes in the living room or the kitchen. "I'll move them," I promised each time. But

I never seemed to get around to doing it. One day when I opened the front door, I found seven pairs of shoes marching across the living room floor headed towards the bedroom. I laughed at my husband's creativity but I also learned to put my shoes away. Your partner's requests to put the toilet seat down, hang up the towel, take the dishes to the sink, or make the bed may seem like picky requests. But think about the message you send your partner when you *don't* make the effort.

Reasonable requests are one thing. But love also means not making unreasonable demands of your partner. It is always okay to ask your partner to change their behavior; it is not okay to ask your partner to change their personality. If your partner is clearly upset, it is not okay to say "get to the point" or "don't cry." Whenever you do make a request, you must ask if your partner feels okay about it. If the answer is no, the loving response is to withdraw the request without anger or recrimination. Otherwise, you are liable to create a situation where your partner feels trapped into making a concession. Again, this is violating your vow to love your partner.

Love also requires you to take care of yourself, physically and emotionally. If you are not your best self, you cannot provide a safe and secure haven for your partner. By not taking care of yourself, you put additional burdens on your partner. Acts of caring can then become dangerously one-sided.

Charles was a diabetic who did not monitor his condition very carefully. His wife Julie was very angry and frustrated by his behavior. On several occasions, she had been called away from work because Charles had been rushed to the hospital when his blood sugar suddenly plunged. Julie also worried that Charles would get into an accident while driving and kill somebody. She took on the daily responsibility of asking him if he had tested himself or had taken his medication.

Their relationship began to resemble a parent/child attachment that undermined their romantic love for each other. Julie thought she had married a man who would provide a secure, loving future. She wanted a true partner and was increasingly angry at Charles' actions. His lack of responsibility, as well as Julie's enabling behavior, almost destroyed their marriage. Once Charles was able to understand how selfish his behavior was, and that it could really cost him his marriage, he began to take ownership of his illness. Julie also had to learn to let go of her hovering and trust that Charles would continue to be a responsible adult.

**Simply put, loving your partner
means never being the
source of their unhappiness.**

Whether the issue is a physical or mental illness, an addiction, an out-of-control temper, or some other issue, doing what you can to manage your problem is necessary if you are to protect your partner from harm. Simply put, loving your partner means never being the source of their unhappiness.

HONOR

Honoring your partner means you are honest at all times and in all things. This means you let your partner know how and what you are feeling, even if it is not pleasant. It means you *do not* avoid an issue because it is disagreeable or makes you uncomfortable. If your partner does something that upsets you, you're not giving them the necessary information to make a change unless you are honest about your concerns. "Stuffing" your feelings only sets your partner up for failure and sets you up for resentment. The need for honesty is not negotiable. Despite what you might wish, the fact that your partner loves you doesn't mean they can read your mind. You have to be willing to tell them how you feel, both good and bad.

Honor means telling your partner about your past, your fears, and your weaknesses, as well as your goals, dreams, and needs. You cannot build a life together, let alone create an *Us*, if you are not completely open about everything. You may be afraid to let your partner know about situations that have hurt you in the past or behaviors you might not be particularly proud of. However, this information allows your partner to understand how you think and why you might behave one way rather than another. You need to be honest so your partner can trust that you are really on board with the plans you make for your future.

Honor also involves letting your partner know what is happening in your daily life. Providing your partner with information about where you are and what you are doing, especially when it affects them, is part of honoring the marriage. Sharing information about daily activities is not about asking permission to do things; it is about honoring your partner's position in your life. If you regularly tell your partner what you are doing and who you're doing it with, doubt and suspicion will never have to crop up. Not sharing this information is lying by omission.

Honoring your partner means you are honest at all times and in all things.

Sharing this way allows your partner a window into your life when you are apart. It also gives your partner the opportunity to share their thoughts and feelings on what you're doing. Open sharing protects your relationship from any outside harm. Establishing these clear lines of communication also lets the world know you are an *Us*. Being open about your commitment to the relationship at all times makes your priorities clear to others in your life.

Honor requires you to be clear with your partner about your feelings, thoughts, likes, and dislikes. It is about honoring your own needs and persisting in trying to get them met in a healthy way. If you aren't honest with your partner about your needs, you are not giving your partner the opportunity to meet them.

Being completely honest in this way is risky, because it requires that you be vulnerable. Most people view vulnerability as a weakness. I respectfully disagree. Being vulnerable means you can handle whatever happens, which means you actually must be quite strong. Being honest requires that strength, and anything less is unfair to your partner and your commitment.

I had the extraordinary honor and privilege of working with a couple who was able to embrace this concept of total honesty in their relationship. When Ron and Catherine came to my office, they were on the brink of ending their 19-year marriage. Ron felt very disconnected from the relationship and wasn't sure the marriage could be saved. Catherine was frustrated as well but they had two children and she wanted to give their marriage every possible chance to survive.

Not only did Ron and Catherine come in twice a month for about six months, they also put a tremendous amount of effort and energy into the relationship outside of sessions. Each took ownership of their part in how the marriage got off track and took on the responsibility to do things differently to put their marriage back on track. Ron and Catherine started to date again on a regular basis. They even developed a Thursday night ritual: dinner and a counseling session. Catherine and Ron began to really talk again. As they spent more time together, Ron and Catherine rekindled their love. They had never been happier or felt more connected when they terminated therapy. "I've never felt more loved and cared for in my entire life," Ron said as they were leaving.

One morning, about six months later, I came into my office

to find the message light on my phone blinking as usual. As I hit the play button, I noticed the time stamp on the first call was 5:30 that morning. I heard Catherine's voice pleading for an emergency appointment. My stomach twisted into a knot. I remembered that Ron had undergone exploratory surgery while they were seeing me. I just knew they were facing a medical dilemma.

When Catherine and Ron walked into my office a few hours later, both of them had red, puffy eyes. Distraught, Ron confessed he'd had a brief affair right before they started seeing me. I almost wished they *were* experiencing a health crisis. Had it been anyone but Ron, I would have really wondered why he would acknowledge an affair that was long over. Ron said, "Things have been so great between us. Holding onto this secret—well, I know what's at stake by telling her, but I can't live with myself if I don't." Ron really felt he was not giving Catherine the opportunity to make a truly informed choice about their marriage.

While Catherine was devastated by her husband's confession, she believed enough in herself and their relationship to be able to consider forgiveness as a real option. Ron's total honesty was difficult for both of them to face but they both recognized that keeping secrets was a violation of the promises they'd made. Ron knew what he was risking by telling Catherine about a past that seemed so far away. But he also knew what was at risk if he didn't.

After crying and talking for an hour and a half, Catherine and Ron were able to focus on how far they had come. They decided, finally, that they weren't willing to lose what they had worked so hard to build. "I know it's going to take some time, and it's not that I'm not tremendously hurt, but I believe Ron. I know that with all we've learned, it will never happen again," Catherine declared. The strong relationship that this couple built was able to withstand one of the worst things that can happen in a marriage. Their promise to honor each other ultimately saved their relationship.

CHERISH

When you cherish your partner, you let them know every day that you care and are glad to have them in your life. You do not take your partner for granted. Cherishing your partner means turning your feelings of love into action. When you wake up in the morning, you ask yourself a simple, powerful question: "How can I make my partner feel loved today?"

**When you cherish your partner,
you let them know every day that you care
and are glad to have them in your life.**

Cherishing your partner means treating them the way you did when you were courting. You do things just because you know they make your partner feel good. You take pride in your appearance and behavior because you want your partner to be proud of you. If your partner feels cherished, they will be a more responsive, loving mate.

Love is really not unconditional. When you act in a way that makes your partner feel cherished, you earn "points" that deepen their love for you. That's just the way human nature works. One of the most important ways you can show how much you cherish your partner is by meeting their emotional needs. You learn to recognize what is important to your partner and you learn to make accommodations to ensure that their needs are met. If one of your partner's needs is affection, making an effort to give them a kiss or a quick hug as you pass by can really make their day. It's a small action that has a large payoff.

Meeting a partner's emotional needs is not an easy or automatic process. All of us tend to act out of habit. You've spent your life doing certain things because they make you feel comfortable. Your partner's request for a change in behavior may bump straight into that comfort zone. When this happens, you may resist change. It's not that you don't want to meet your partner's needs. It's just that it takes extra effort and attention on your part. However, if you don't meet those needs despite repeated requests, your partner may come to believe you don't care much about their comfort and happiness. Worse yet, your partner may come to believe that they don't matter to you. Once this happens, your partner will begin to withdraw from the relationship. They will start to care less about you.

Valerie came to see me alone because she was unhappy with herself and her marriage. Her husband, Frank, refused to come because he was "fine" with the relationship and thought she was the one with the problem.

The child of two alcoholics, Valerie grew up in a world of chaos. Neither parent could hold a job for long, so Valerie got used to coming home to an empty refrigerator or, worse, an eviction notice on the door. When she met Frank, she refused to become involved with him until she could trust that he had a stable job and personal life. Valerie wanted to know if he had an apartment, his own car, and how long he had been in his job. When Frank started to work for the state as a software engineer, Valerie believed she could finally have the secure life she'd always craved. She married him.

While Valerie was pregnant with their second child, Frank decided he wanted to branch out and start his own software firm. She tried hard to be supportive, but her old fears oozed back. "Every month, when I sit down to pay the bills, I start to panic as the balance gets closer to zero. Sometimes, I think I can even hear the sheriff's deputy stepping onto the porch," Valerie stated sadly. While Frank had always known about his wife's need for stability, he thought Valerie was overreacting. "We've never missed paying a bill on time. I don't understand why she is afraid now," Frank complained. In fact, his business did begin to thrive, and Valerie was able to relax.

Then, the economy took off and a larger company bought out Frank's business. "I'm going to take a few months off to relax and figure out what I want to do next," he told Valerie. Since they had substantial savings, Valerie reluctantly agreed they could manage for a while.

As time passed, Frank decided he didn't want to work for any-one else. He also didn't want to go through the difficulty of starting another company. Three months of vacation turned into a year. Every month, as Valerie paid the bills and watched their savings diminish, she became increasingly anxious. When she tried to talk with Frank about their financial circumstances and the anxiety she was feeling, Frank would dismiss her with assurances "that every-thing would work out."

But when the bottom fell out of the stock market, Valerie and Frank lost a third of the value of their investments. To complicate matters, their eldest child was due to start college, with the second one just a year behind. At present, Frank is still unemployed and Valerie feels increasingly hurt and angry. Frank's refusal to take Valerie's need for financial security seriously and stretch beyond his comfort zone to meet her need is causing serious damage to their relationship. Despite attending several therapy sessions and recognizing his wife's need for stability, Frank is at a loss to under-stand why she no longer wants to spend time with him. Sadly, he does not recognize that he holds the key to the success of his own marriage.

One of the predictable consequences of couples failing to cherish each other is that they grow apart. So often I hear my couple clients say "we've become two different people." This is a direct result of not keeping the vow to cherish each other daily. Cherishing requires openness and flexibility. Your partner is not

> **You need to continually learn about
> your partner's needs, just as your partner
> must keep learning about yours.**

going to remain the same over time and neither are you. Their interests, activities, and needs will change over the years you are together. If you're not paying attention and acting with intention in relation to those changes, you'll have trouble accommodating your partner. So, you need to continually learn about your partner's needs, just as your partner must keep learning about yours. Each of you may need to develop new behaviors and habits over time, in accordance with your partner's changing needs. At times, this can be challenging. But your willingness to participate in this process allows you to keep the vital promise you made to cherish each other.

DEFINING FEATURES OF THE *Us*

A few years back, I attended the wedding of a good friend. It was his third and I was trying my best to believe that this one would take. One part of the ceremony really touched my sense of hope for the future of this marriage—and if taken to heart, other marriages. The minister chose not to read the frequently quoted passage about the first marriage at Cana. Instead, he quoted Colossians 3:12, "Therefore, as God's chosen people, holy and dearly loved, clothe yourself with compassion, kindness, humility, gentleness and patience." His message was simple: if we exhibit these qualities toward our partners, our marriages will be healthier and happier. How easily this approach gets lost in day-to-day living! Granted, these behaviors don't always come as easily as we would wish. However, if you and your partner can include them in your definition of *Us*, you will create a lasting pattern of love and respect. Let's take a closer look at the key features of the *Us*.

COMPASSION is the feeling aroused when we see a hurt child or animal. It is what drives our efforts to help those less fortunate than ourselves. Remember how we responded in the days following 9/11 and Hurricane Katrina? Many of us were driven to give of ourselves to relieve the suffering of others in whatever way we could. Sometimes we forget that this sense of compassion is needed much closer to home. If you are able to reach inside and express the same sense of caring and concern for your partner as you often do for strangers, your partner will feel a sense of security that will deepen the relationship.

KINDNESS is doing things for your partner that make them feel good. It is meeting your partner's needs with a joyful spirit, not a sense of duty. Kindness calls upon your ability to step outside yourself and put your partner first. You would be showing kindness by making the bed for your partner when they are running late. It's also when you fold your partner's laundry and put it away before you check your e-mail.

Kindness is also present when you give your partner the benefit of the doubt about their intentions. When your partner doesn't tell you that your mother called, you show kindness by accepting their explanation that they truly forgot and not that they dislike your mother. The wonderful thing about kindness is that it is highly contagious. Kindness breeds kindness. Every small act of warmth and understanding toward your partner will return to you tenfold. It's as though you are making small love deposits into your relationship and providing it with an ongoing cushion of support.

HUMILITY is the ability to admit that you don't have all the answers. It is the capacity to acknowledge that you don't do everything right. Humility is what allows you to apologize to your partner without feeling diminished or inferior. If no one is right, no one has to be wrong. When you are humble you are able to hear your partner's position without having to defend your own.

This openness allows for the kind of free, loving communication that builds the foundation for a successful relationship.

GENTLENESS displaces anger in the relationship. It allows the loving feelings that keep a marriage alive to be nurtured. When you are gentle with your partner, you provide a safe place to discuss any issue that may arise. It removes any sense of fear or anxiety that might prevent the development of a truly honest and intimate relationship. Gentleness can protect a couple from the storms life may bring. It sets the tone for a sense of peace and harmony in the relationship.

PATIENCE may be the most essential of the *Us* behaviors. Patience gives your partner permission to be different from you. When you're patient, you're able to take a step back and examine a situation objectively, distanced from your immediate emotional reactions. Patience permeates your relationship with an overall sense of calm. It allows for issues to be resolved over time, when the best opportunity arises to find an optimal solution. Marriages built on a foundation of patience will have the strength to withstand the stresses that inevitably arise in a long-term relationship.

FINAL THOUGHTS

Developing and practicing these behaviors in your marriage enables the commitment you have made to each other to take root. When this commitment is present and active, you and your partner will feel free to address any issues or concerns that may arise with a sense of safety and common purpose. You will never have to avoid a problem out of fear of a bad outcome. You will never be unhappily surprised by each other's response or afraid of each other's reaction because you will have established groundrules that will ensure the success of your relationship.

SUGGESTED DESIGN ACTIVITIES

The following questions are meant to help you and your partner honor your marriage vows on a daily basis. Learning to act in specific, intentional ways that support your relationship will help it to both survive and thrive.

1. How do you show your partner that you love them? How does your partner show you love?

2. Are you always honest with your partner? When are you inclined not to be?

3. How do you make your partner feel safe enough to tell you their innermost thoughts and feelings? How does your partner make you feel secure enough to do the same?

4. What do you do to make your partner feel cherished? How do they make you feel cherished?

5. Using the above model for the *Us*, define how you and your partner will begin to include these features in your marriage blueprint.

CHAPTER 5

ROOF OF THE *Us*:
STAY CONNECTED

Chains do not hold a marriage together.
It is threads, hundreds of tiny threads,
which sew people together through the years.
That is what makes a marriage—
more than passion or even sex!

– Simone Signoret, actress

Couples usually come to see me because they are having some kind of difficulty in their relationship. Some couples come in for what I call "hard" reasons, such as adultery, drug or alcohol use, verbal or physical abuse, etc. But most couples come into therapy for "soft" reasons: the couple has grown apart, they don't communicate anymore, or one partner is no longer "in love" with their partner. Many of these soft reasons have a common root cause. *The two individuals are no longer connected to each other.*

When you become disconnected from your partner, your relationship can begin to deteriorate. You each become wrapped up in your own world. *Your* job, *your* interests, *your* desires become paramount, while those of your partner take a back seat. As a result, you and your partner become less comfortable in each other's presence. Conversations become strained and limited to exchanges of information instead of goal-oriented dialogs that focus on plans, feelings, or resolving issues that allow for deeper connection with your partner. Exchanges that were once considered playful, teasing, and fun-filled interplay are taken as serious opinion. As a result, you and your partner avoid each other even more, and the relationship continues to spiral downward.

For many couples, part of the problem is time—or rather the lack of it. With all of the daily demands and pressures people face today, spending quality time as a couple often falls by the wayside. You and your partner's focus may be diverted by work, children, household responsibilities, extended family demands, and other obligations. Everything is rush, rush, rush and by the end of the day, you and your partner may simply do what "needs" to be done and then collapse. Long gone are the hours spent focused on each other and the relationship. You and your partner may give each other a peck on the cheek in the morning and before bed, maybe watch a show together on television, and think everything is okay.

The problem with this pattern is that you're not building up any reserves in your relationship. So when you run into any difficulty you and your partner don't have a reservoir of good feeling and sense of common purpose to handle it. Every time one of you brings up a particular issue, you restate your same positions, try to convince your partner of the clarity of your thinking or the fallacy of theirs, become defensive, and either argue or shut down. Since you and your partner can't ever seem to resolve the issue, you become even more tense around each other and, as a result, spend even less time together. Eventually, it may become difficult for you and your partner to have even the most superficial conversations.

If you and your partner can't talk about everyday things in an easy manner, you will never be able to address anything more serious about your relationship. The inability to manage your relationship in a healthy and productive way leads to a disconnection between you and your partner. This disconnection leads to difficulties in all aspects of the relationship, from deciding how and where to spend your time to levels of physical intimacy.

Tim and Beth came to my office because they had been fighting almost nonstop. Their sex life was pretty much nonexistent. Both were very career-oriented and spent a lot of time at work. When they were at home, Tim spent his time in the study playing an on-line role-playing game, while Beth sat in the living room watching romantic movies on the Lifetime channel. Their "dates" consisted of picking up take-out on the way home. When I suggested that they might want to try spending some more time together, they immediately resisted.

Tim began his challenge statement with, "My marriage is important but ..." He went on to talk about the demands of work, the limited time he had for himself, tasks he wanted to get done around the house, and, basically, everything else he could think of that made it impossible to make time for his wife. Tim ended by saying, "Stuff just comes up."

Tim was missing a very important point. You teach people what's important to you by how you spend your time. If you tell someone your relationship with them is important to you but you never seem to have time for them, your words will start to ring hollow. We all know that if we don't show up for our jobs, we will get fired. The same thing will happen if you aren't present for your marriage. You will lose your partner.

THE BIOCHEMISTRY OF LOVE

When you began to date—and particularly when you begin to define yourself as a couple—you and your partner undoubtedly spent a lot of time together. You went out to dinner, to the movies, shopping. You devoted time and energy planning your life together, sharing your goals, hopes, and dreams. You also probably felt an unmistakable electricity and physical attraction to each other. You made the time to be together because defining your relationship was important to you both.

Then, as time went on, you and your partner may have begun to fall into the habit of not making specific plans to do things as a couple. While this tendency to "drift" is normal, it is not in the long-term interest of your relationship. It is natural for you and your partner to count on the other always being there, but you have to be careful not to take each other for granted.

The type of relationship we have with our partner when we first fall in love is all-enveloping. But *why* is the early phase of love so all-encompassing, and why does it change? Early on, a combination of physiological and psychological processes motivate human beings to meet, mate, and procreate, thus ensuring the survival of the species. When you become attracted to someone, and start to fall in love, your brain releases dopamine. This is a natural chemical that makes you feel good and is responsible for your bright outlook on life. These effects last approximately 18 to 36 months because our bodies are not designed to function in that heightened state for longer than that. After that, the continued existence of the relationship depends on the development of a more mature and meaningful connection. This connection still requires focus and attention, but of a different kind.

MAKING TIME

Chad and Ellen have been married for 20 years. For their entire marriage, Chad has traveled almost every week for his job. When their children were small, Ellen took on most of the responsibility for raising them. Chad did what he could but was limited by the brief periods of time he was home. Now the children are grown and Ellen has returned to the workforce. Recently, she has found that staying connected to Chad has become more difficult.

In particular, Ellen has noticed the strain of reconnecting when Chad returns from a trip. To lessen this strain, they've worked out a plan where Chad calls her every morning while she is driving to work, but it doesn't feel like enough for Ellen. She has asked him to please call her at least one other time during the day. Usually, Chad tries to call around dinnertime, but often he feels pressed if he has an upcoming meeting with clients or other work demands. He frequently will preface the conversation with, "I don't have much time to talk." This makes Ellen feel not only unimportant, but also that she is a burden to her husband. Once Chad understood that Ellen just wanted a quick check-in to feel connected, not a long, drawn-out conversation, he learned to stop mentioning how little time he had and just be present for the time he did have.

Take a moment to think about how you interact with your partner now. Do you call each other during the day? Make plans to get together for a meal? Set aside time to participate in activities you are both interested in? Do you talk about your day? Share your hopes and dreams for the future? If so, you and your partner are connecting on a frequent basis that allows you to have a deeper, more passionate relationship. It is this type of connection that will see you through if, and more likely when, things get a bit rough between the two of you.

When you and your partner make time on a regular basis to talk and share activities you both enjoy, it is like vaccinating your relationship against the twin diseases of complacency and distance. These two disorders can infect a relationship unless care is taken to protect it. It is easy to fall into a pattern in which you focus on the mundane day-to-day tasks and events and fail to recognize the symptoms of disconnection happening between you and your partner.

It is easy to fall into a pattern in which you focus on the mundane day-to-day tasks and events and fail to recognize the symptoms of disconnection happening between you and your partner.

It's important that you and your partner continue to make time to be together. It doesn't need to be fancy or expensive, but it does need to be regular. This point reminds me of an experience I had when I was a teenager. It stuck with me because it was something I never saw happen in my own home. I had spent the night with a friend whose parents maintained an unbreakable Friday night tradition. My friend's mom would feed the three girls early and send them off to entertain themselves. She then would carefully set the dining room table with their fine china surrounding a centerpiece of fresh flowers. When her husband got home, she would light the candles and serve their dinner. The couple then had some quiet, uninterrupted time to catch up on what was happening in each other's lives.

The only time my parents ate in the dining room was either when they had a dinner party or we were having a holiday dinner. I don't remember them ever eating alone as a couple. Later, I realized that by taking this time to be alone together, my friend's parents could address issues of all types, from the mundane to the playful to the serious. This dining ritual gave them the opportunity to address things in the relationship before they became problematic. The focus was on each other and, therefore, their relationship remained alive and healthy.

Edward and Donna came to see me when they were engaged to make sure they got off on the right foot. Donna had been married before and didn't want to fail at another relationship. Edward's previous relationships had been relatively short-lived. When he started to feel that he was expected to change to make his partner

79

happy, he would end the relationship. Edward was concerned that he was incapable of making a serious commitment to anyone.

In therapy, Donna and Edward worked very hard to understand what issues set each of them off, as well as the ways each of them engaged in unproductive behaviors when upset. The day they came in and told me they had set a wedding date was one of the most rewarding I'd ever experienced as a therapist. Later, looking at the pictures of the happy couple during their sunset wedding ceremony on the sandy Jamaican beach, I felt renewed in my sense of hope and optimism for the work I do.

Of course, the wedding is only the beginning. Donna and Edward continued to see me about once a month for continuing checkups. A major concern was that both had high-pressure jobs that required lots of travel. Frequently, they didn't see each other for days at a time. After about six months of marriage they found themselves sniping at each other for small things and blowing up whenever they tried to discuss anything of real importance.

However, Donna and Edward reported that when they went on vacation together, things were very different. "How different?" I asked. The couple acknowledged that, on vacation, they were able to be together without the real world interfering. "We had chunks of time to just talk about anything we wanted, from what we would do that day, to what each of us wanted out of life and everything in between," Donna said with a smile. Edward added that sometimes they didn't talk at all but just quietly enjoyed being in each other's company. They told me that these moments brought back to them why they'd wanted to be married in the first place. "What you've discovered," I told them, "is the power of staying connected."

THE IMPORTANCE OF RITUALS

Unfortunately, most of us can't live our lives on perpetual vacation with all the time in the world and no responsibilities. This is where the importance of developing rituals comes in. Rituals are those patterns of behavior we create that serve as a kind of shorthand for staying connected. My friend's parents' weekly dinner date was a ritual. So is how you leave each other each morning and how you greet each other when you return in the evening. Anything you do that keeps you close both physically and emotionally can be a ritual.

Donna and Edward discovered their mutual fondness for kayaking on slow-moving rivers. They now make time to go kayaking together at least once a month. It gives them time on the way to talk about the everyday stuff and then to enjoy the outdoors and each other while on the river. Frequently, the conversation turns deeper and more profound on the way home. This single ritual has guaranteed them time to reinforce their connection. Edward and Donna are trying to create other rituals to ensure the success of their relationship.

Creating love rituals is another way to stay connected over time. A love ritual is any behavior that tells your partner they are special to you. It can be an act as simple as making a dish that your partner especially likes, to buying a single rose in your partner's favorite color, to sticking a note or card in your partner's suitcase when they travel. I have always gotten nervous before I take a test or give a presentation. When I was in graduate school, my husband devised a love ritual that never failed to make me smile and let me know he cared. I would leave the house a bundle of nerves, jump into the car, and find a yellow sticky note on the steering wheel with the words "Go get 'em" or "Knock 'em dead." This simple act let me know that my husband was aware of my schedule and that he was my biggest cheerleader.

Going to bed together on a regular basis is another love ritual you and your partner can implement. It gives you time to wind down at the end of the day, engage in couple time, and allows you to focus solely on each other. This means making time to have conversations about each of your days, deeper conversations about something you learned that relates to one of your goals or dreams. It also means, of course, making love when the mood is right.

**It's important to make time to
have fun on a regular basis.**

Another ritual couples can institute to help them stay connected is "date night." It's important to still make time to have fun on a regular basis. Whether you go out or plan to spend time at home as a couple, it's essential for the *Us* to have specific time set aside each week to just be together without children, other family members, or anyone else. This time is for talking about dreams, goals, vacation plans, a story you read in the paper or heard on the radio, or some other idea you wish to share with your partner. It's also time to laugh, flirt, and just have fun.

What is off the table on date night is any discussion about your work, the children, or what's *not* going right in the relationship. This time should be spent learning about your partner's opinions, world view, and desires, and for your partner to learn about yours. Put date night on your weekly schedule and treat it as a sacred activity that is sacrificed only for emergencies.

Another ritual that helps couples stay connected is a weekly "couple confab." Again, this is a specific time on your weekly schedule when you and your partner discuss the status of your relationship. Just like a meeting at work, this contained conversation has a defined agenda and time frame, usually no more than an hour. It needs to be scheduled at a time when you and your partner can give each other your undivided attention. This means you both need to be rested and focused, with any child care issues taken care of. It's a time to take the relationship's temperature, talk about what's working, and where you might make any adjustments.

The couples confab is a regular opportunity to address how your needs—and those of your partner—are being met. In this forum, you can make reasonable and rational requests for a change in your partner's behavior. You and your partner can have ongoing discussions about any issues or concerns that either of you has about your life together. It is also the time to evaluate or address any alterations that need to be made to the guidelines of your *Us*.

FINAL THOUGHTS

By making specific plans to spend time with your partner and to be consciously present in the relationship, you will stay grounded in what made you want to marry your partner in the first place. You will be able to catch potential problems more quickly and have a plan in place to handle them before they have a chance to spin out of control and cause real damage. By taking the time to stay connected to your partner, you give yourselves the ability to grow together as a loving and intimate *Us*.

In addition, by keeping in close touch with your partner, you will always be able to give them the benefit of the doubt when a disagreement or miscommunication arises. Because you will know how your partner thinks and behaves, you will be secure in the knowledge of their good intentions. You will also have a concrete strategy that allows quick resolution of any potential problem.

SUGGESTED DESIGN ACTIVITIES

These questions are designed to get you and your partner focused on keeping your relationship front and center. They are meant to help you manage the everyday events and still pay attention to your marriage.

1. What did you and your partner regularly do when dating?

2. How can you incorporate at least one of these activities into your current relationship?

3. What challenges get in the way of you and your partner spending one-on-one time together?

4. What rituals have you and your partner established for connecting on a daily basis? What rituals would you like to establish?

5. Establish regular times for date night and couple confabs.

CHAPTER 6

THE FLOW OF THE *Us*: COLLABORATE, DON'T COMPETE

Many marriages would be better if the husband and the wife clearly understood that they are on the same side.

– Zig Ziglar, author & motivational speaker

A commonly accepted position is that marriage is a 50/50 proposition. In fact, for a relationship to be successful, each partner is 100% responsible for its success. To have a truly great relationship you must be willing to live the marriage vows you took without regard to what your partner is doing.

Your commitment to being the best partner possible, with the focus on *your* behavior, will allow your relationship to reach its greatest potential as a cooperative partnership. You may be thinking, "But what about my partner? It's not fair that I have to be the one to make all the effort." The reason is because, in reality, the only person whose behavior you have any control over is your own. If you are focused on the actions of your partner, it is impossible to take ownership of your own behaviors. And by being 100% responsible for yourself, and letting your partner do the same, you make it possible to have a truly cooperative relationship.

Part of this commitment to cooperation is giving your partner the benefit of the doubt, unless you have facts to the contrary. This means if your partner's explanation can fit the circumstances as you know them, you accept it. If it's possible your partner's meeting ran late or their cell phone died, take your partner's word. Continuing to believe that your partner is acting from a position of care and consideration frees you to focus on your own expressions of love and commitment.

Focusing on the failures of the other provides an excuse not to focus on what is really the primary responsibility of both: making sure each of you is being the best partner possible.

When two people decide to join their lives together and establish a committed relationship, they usually begin from a place of trust in the other's best intentions. But over time, this willingness to give one's partner the benefit of the doubt tends to fade. You begin to feel that your partner is no longer concerned with putting forth the effort to keep the relationship strong. Both of you start to focus more on what you're *not getting* from the relationship rather than what each of you *is doing* to ensure its successful future. This focus on the failures of the other provides each of you with the excuse to not focus on what is really the primary responsibility of both: making sure each of you is being the best partner possible.

Madeline came to my office with her husband Bruce in tow. She bluntly stated, "If you would just 'fix' him, the relationship would be just fine." It was a statement I'd heard from one partner or the other many times before. Calmly, I pointed out that Bruce was not "broken" and that each of them had to take ownership of how their marriage had gotten off track. I also let them know that continuing to focus on what each partner was *not* doing would keep the relationship on its downward spiral. "By hanging onto what you're not getting," I said, "you give yourself permission to not give to your partner."

But Madeline continued to be quite self-righteous in her insistence that the trouble in her marriage was all Bruce's fault. She didn't want to see the truth: by putting the entire responsibility for the relationship in Bruce's lap, Madeline was avoiding the work of stepping up to the plate and participating fully in their marriage. Unfortunately, Madeline continued her focus on Bruce's "failings" until he gave up trying. He filed for divorce six months later.

What happened with Madeline and Bruce is an example of what philosophers call self-deception. In *Leadership and Self-Deception,* the Arbinger Institute defines self-deception as "the inability to see that one has a problem." Madeline was only able to see things from her closed perspective. She was also highly resistant to the idea that the truth about her and Bruce's problems was different from what she believed. In addition, no matter how someone is acting towards us on the outside, most of us can tell how others really feel about us and that's what we respond to. Bruce eventually responded to Madeline's true feelings about him by leaving the relationship.

THE HARM OF COMPETITION

One way that lack of trust and doubt in your partner can occur is if the two of you start competing with each other. Remember Tom and Maggie from Chapter 2? He took the position that if he did what Maggie wanted she would win, which is an example of competition in a relationship. If you and your partner set up your relationship in terms of winning and losing like Tom and Maggie, you are implicitly working against each other and this contradicts the concept of the *Us.*

Competition can show up in relationships in many ways. They include, but are not limited to, the following:

✦   Whose job takes priority?

+ Who makes more money?

+ Who has gotten more promotions?

+ Who looks better?

+ Who deserves to have things done that makes them feel good?

+ Who gets to do things they like?

+ Who is the better parent?

+ Who has more friends?

How you and your partner address these issues will determine how much you each of you feels loved and cared for.

When partners are motivated by winning, or getting their way, the focus of the relationship is on the individual, not the couple. Partners caught in this cycle engage in scorekeeping; each one keeps careful track of what they have done for the other and, more to the point, what the other has *not* done. Each time your partner "scores" a point against you, your focus becomes finding a way to "even the score." Marriage research has shown that it takes five positive interactions to counteract a single negative one. But if a couple perpetually keeps score, it's likely that they're going to build up a lot of resentment and, in turn, express more negative than positive feelings.

Looking at how this process gets started requires a return to the concept of self-deception. This process starts with an act of self-betrayal and proceeds downhill from there. According to the Arbinger Institute, this is a seven-step process that proceeds as follows:

1. Self-betrayal is acting in opposition to what you feel you should do for another person, e.g., your partner.

2. Once you "betray" yourself, you begin to see the world in a way that justifies that self-betrayal.

3. When you see a self-justifying world, your view of reality becomes distorted.

4. When you betray yourself you become locked into your view of distorted reality.

5. Over time, certain views of the world become characteristic of you and you carry them with you.

6. By having certain views, you trigger others to hold to certain views of their own.

7. Once there, the two of you invite continued mutual mistreatment and engage in mutual justification.
   In other words, you conspire to maintain your own distorted views.

Engaging in this process of self-betrayal and self-deception is at the very heart of how couples go from being all about behaving in ways that support the relationship to "What has my partner done for me lately?" Once you begin to focus on your partner's faults and the ways they annoy you, the process of falling out of love has begun. The way to keep your relationship on track is to learn how to work as a team at all times and in all ways.

In his book, *His Needs, Her Needs*, Dr. Willard Harley talks about the importance of each partner's "love bank." Each partner interprets the other's behavior as either "deposits" or "withdrawals" into their personal love account. When either of you is focused on the size of the deposits in your own love bank and not the size of the balance in your partner's account, your attention is on the wrong thing. If you are not consciously and continuously adding to your partner's love bank, it will eventually drop to zero. Whoever reaches zero first will begin to wonder whether the relationship holds any value and whether it is worth continuing.

One way couples engage in competition is with their finances. Most partners don't make the same amount of money, which already puts one person ahead. If the couple decides to keep their money separate and divide the bills instead, things can get even more complicated. When one partner is responsible for certain bills and not others it allows that partner to determine that they have completed their responsibilities to the household and are now free to spend any of the remaining money. The other partner may be struggling financially but, since the couple has not established a collaborative approach, the problem becomes that partner's to solve.

Ellen and Jake had been living together for a year when Ellen came to see me. While they were not yet engaged, they had talked about getting married on several occasions. But Ellen was worried because Jake had purchased the home they were living in and she was not on the deed. Ellen and Jake split the bills: he paid for the mortgage and some of the other bills, while she paid the rest. Ellen made much less money than Jake and could not contribute financially for some of the household items they wanted. Ellen really wanted a certain table for the living room but couldn't afford it herself. She was not at all comfortable asking Jake to buy it. She was a bit resentful because he had purchased a new, state-of-the-art computer for his study from his additional funds while the living room looked barren. She wanted to marry him, and they eventually did get engaged, but Ellen did not feel as if she and Jake had started as partners. Ellen and Jake changed the way they handled their money once they married. Both took responsibility for all household expenses.

Another way that disparate salaries can cause a couple difficulties is by influencing the self-worth of one of the partners. Sam and Stephanie have been married for over ten years. They disagree all the time about money. Stephanie has it and Sam doesn't. Like Jake and Ellen, they also split the bills and Sam frequently has difficulty paying "his" bills. He works as a waiter and doesn't have a set income. He feels humiliated when he has to "ask" Stephanie to help him out. Even though he doesn't think he buys into the "man as provider" stereotype, it affects how he feels about himself as a man. He doesn't feel he is an equal partner in the relationship.

Recently, Sam returned to college to be able to have a career as a surgical nurse. Even though as a couple Sam and Stephanie have the money to pay the tuition, Sam feels that he has to come up with it himself. Even though his new career would be moving both of them toward the life they want, Stephanie feels no responsibility for helping Sam achieve his dream. If they had a truly collaborative relationship, both would take ownership of Sam's goal of improving himself *and* responsibility for life's expenses.

This concept of "his and her money" is just one of the many ways couples compete instead of collaborate. Choosing whose career is more important is another way. A colleague of mine, Theresa, recently faced just this decision with her husband David. David was offered a promotion that required him to move to corporate headquarters, which is located in another state. However, Theresa had recently opened her therapy practice and it was beginning to take off. Unfortunately, the state where the corporate headquarters is located did not offer reciprocal licensing for Theresa. Moving meant that she would have to close down her business, get more training, and go through the licensing process again. After four years of hard work, Theresa would have to spend more time and money to get where she was right now. After they had talked openly and at length about this dilemma, David agreed that the move didn't make sense for them as a couple. He would just have to find another way to move forward in his company. He chose collaboration over competition.

Intimacy is another arena where couples compete instead of working as a team. Men and women frequently get into a power struggle in some area of their relationship. They engage in continual back and forth, you versus me, "my way or the highway" interactions. This pervasive tension creates distance in the couple. They subsequently play out this struggle for power and control by withholding intimacy from each other. This may not seem like competition but it is. When one person feels like they are "losing," the response is often one of "oh yeah, take this." The other partner then feels like they are losing and retaliates in kind. The foundation of safety and security needed for real intimacy to occur gets lost and the *Us* begins to crumble. Loss of intimacy takes many forms, from not having deep discussions about goals and dreams to lack of sexual relations. If you are competing with your partner over whose need for intimacy gets met, and under what circumstances, you are playing a highly risky game of chicken.

One form of competition in this area springs from lack of knowledge as opposed to intentional action. Men often don't make the connection between affection and getting their sexual needs met. They don't understand that the purpose of conversation and nonsexual touch for a woman is to set the stage for romance. Many men only hug or touch their partners with sexual intimacy as the goal. Women then learn that the only time their partner really talks to them or touches them is when the man wants sex.

As a result, many women begin to reject their partners' advances. Many men respond by becoming more insistent and less inviting, while their partners increasingly pull away. Each partner interprets this unproductive pattern in terms of how their needs are or, more to the point, are not being met. It then becomes a classic case of one partner seeking to get what they want without regard to the effect on the other partner. This entire scenario can be avoided by joining together as a team, focusing on attaining mutually determined goals, and working with each other to achieve them.

THE BENEFITS OF COLLABORATION

The entire premise of the *Us* is based on the concept of moving from two individuals focused on satisfying their own needs to establishing a genuine partnership. In this kind of collaborative partnership, success is measured by how well both the relationship and each partner are doing. The idea is simple: individuals only win if the relationship is winning. If either individual is not doing well, by definition the relationship is losing. It is the same concept that drives an athletic team or a business. Each individual has a role to play, but the game requires all the players to do their jobs to achieve victory. One individual might excel, but if their actions prevent other key plays or deals from being made, the result will be a net loss. Marriage is the ultimate team game. Both partners must put forth their best efforts to achieve a winning record.

**The entire premise of the *Us*
is that individuals only win
if the relationship is winning.**

Victor and Maria came to see me just after they got engaged. Maria had been married before, while this would be Victor's first. They came for counseling because they wanted to "get their marriage right." Both had strong religious beliefs and took the idea of marriage very seriously. But Victor, like a lot of people, was afraid of committing to one person for the rest of his life. His track record with relationships hadn't been very good and he was concerned he wouldn't be successful this time either.

Victor and Maria were filled with excitement and hope the day they told me they had set a wedding date. It meant they both believed they had dealt with their commitment concerns and were ready to move forward together as a couple. The wedding went off without a hitch, and Victor and Maria seemed to be very happy with each other and with the relationship. They still came in to see me about once a month to negotiate the inevitable bumps that come with the transition to marriage.

One of the recurring issues they brought in was how to communicate more effectively. Maria liked to examine a topic from all angles and in great detail. Victor just wanted to get to the bottom line and resolve the issue. Maria was always trying to get Victor to tell her how he felt about things and what he wanted to do. She expressed annoyance with always being the one to have to make a decision about where they went and what they did. "Why is it always up to me to decide what we have for dinner or what movie we see?" Maria complained. "I just want Victor to take some ownership in our relationship."

Victor took Maria's suggestion to heart and made a great effort to let his wife know either what his preferences were or that he really didn't care. He also tried to find out her preferences before trying to make decisions that would involve both of them.

Unfortunately, he found himself in a catch 22: Maria found that being asked about her preferences before Victor stated his was annoying as well. Maria acknowledged that Victor could not read her mind and that she really did appreciate how seriously he had taken her request. "I can see how important it is to Victor that I'm happy," Maria said one day. "He makes such an effort to be accommodating." She thought about how important the success of their marriage was to both of them and realized she needed to focus on that instead of her annoyance. Both Victor and Maria put the good of the team ahead of their own "hot button" emotional reactions.

FINAL THOUGHTS

It is a maxim that a single stick is relatively easy to break. However, if a couple of sticks are bundled together, it takes much greater force to break them. The same holds true for a relationship. If you and your partner stand alone—or worse, actively compete with each other—your relationship is vulnerable to breaking under even a small strain. However, if you and your partner stand together as a collaborative team and "have each other's backs," your relationship should be able to handle even the most difficult challenge.

SUGGESTED DESIGN ACTIVITIES

Now may be a good time to examine how you and your partner might be competing with each other. The following questions are designed to help you and your partner develop a more collaborative relationship.

1. How do you and your partner compete?

2. What causes you and your partner to struggle for power?

3. When and how do you keep score in the relationship?

4. How do you and your partner collaborate in your relationship?

5. What would help you and your partner work together better and more often?

CHAPTER 7

THE AMENITIES OF THE *Us*:
MEET YOUR PARTNER'S NEEDS

Real giving is when we give to our spouses what's
important to them, whether we understand it,
like it, agree with it, or not.

– Michele Weiner-Davis, author & therapist

In discussing the creation of the *Us*, I addressed the step of identifying who you are and what you need. Knowing what your needs are and ensuring they are met is important. Equally important is recognizing your partner's needs and then willingly meeting them. When you and your partner began as a couple, you both probably spent many hours trying to find ways to make each other happy. You looked for the ideal gift, wore the outfit that your partner found so attractive, or created the perfect date that would always be special to the two of you.

What you were doing then was identifying and meeting your partner's most important needs. You were also making your partner feel like a priority in your life. Continuing to do this means providing those little touches in your relationship that will make it safe, comfortable, and homey—a place where you both will always want to be. It's the extra-special touches that will make it completely yours.

The minute you stop meeting your partner's needs, the connection between you breaks down and your relationship becomes vulnerable.

Since human beings are communal creatures, one of our requirements is the need for togetherness, or being connected to others. This is the need most of us are trying to meet while dating. Unfortunately, we don't all need the same amount of togetherness or require that the need be met in the same way. While dating, we are learning about another person and deciding if the information we gather makes us want to move closer to that person, or further away. In other words, dating allows you to find out whether this person can meet your particular needs and vice versa. If each of you can meet the other's needs, the relationship continues; if not, it ends. This is why it's essential to continue to meet your partner's needs over the course of the relationship. The minute you stop meeting your partner's needs, the connection between you breaks down and your relationship becomes vulnerable.

The problem most of us face is that even if we know what our needs are, we may not always know how to get them met. One way of addressing this issue is to identify the times in your life when you were happiest. Most likely, one or more of your most important needs were being met. The more specific you can be about what was happening at that time, the clearer you can be about what works for getting your needs met.

The next step is to let your partner know what you need in order to feel safe and secure in the relationship. When we talk about *needs* these are distinct from *wants*. Wants are things you *prefer to have* but can negotiate around, such as where you would like to live. Needs are things you *must have* to feel complete and confident in the relationship, such as feeling that you matter as a person. Needs cannot be compromised, but how they are met can be negotiated.

At the beginning of our relationship we are usually very focused on what it takes to make our partner happy. Unfortunately, we tend to gradually move from doing what makes our partner happy to an attitude of "What have they done for me lately?" Once you move in this direction, you have stopped focusing on the *Us* and have returned to the lens of the individual. One way to avoid this shift is to make a conscious effort to meet your partner's needs. While you shouldn't do this with the intent that your needs will be met in return, this is the most likely outcome. When a person feels content and secure, it is much easier to focus outside the self. In this way, giving tends to generate giving.

You can only get inside your own head and be clear about what you need. As a result, all of us have a tendency to assume that if we feel a certain way about something, our partner will feel the same. A great example of this is how you express your love for someone else. If you need to hear the words "I love you," you will most likely say those words to your partner. If your partner needs to hear these words as well, it's wonderful. But it's not so good if the way your partner feels your love is when you do something thoughtful and unexpected for them, like plan a delicious dinner when you know they have had a rough day. If you simply assume that your partner needs love expressed exactly the way you do, and you act accordingly, there may be serious miscommunication and hurt feelings.

The bottom line: people are different from each other. Something may be very important to you but not even register as a blip on your partner's radar screen. Therefore, it is essential that your partner knows not only the importance of your need, but more importantly, how to meet it. I know this takes the romance out of the idea that you and your partner are so in tune that your partner can read your mind. However, if your partner has to guess about what will make you happy and content, the chances of hitting the bull's eye every time is very slim. What is bound to result is resentment on your part and confusion on your partner's.

> **If your partner has to guess about what will make you happy and content, the chances of hitting the bull's eye every time is very slim.**

So you ask, "Okay, I have identified my need and how I prefer it to be met. I have shared this information with my partner. Now what?" This is where the concept of the *Us* comes into play. Your emotional needs and the emotional needs of your partner become the emotional needs of the *Us*. If you are both focused on meeting the needs of the *Us*, instead of just getting your own needs met, then you are putting the success of your partnership first.

Sometimes this involves giving up something you might *want* to do at a particular moment in order to meet one of your partner's needs. For example, you might record a favorite TV show or athletic event you really wanted to watch to talk with your partner about a particularly difficult experience they had that day. However, if you do this out of love, and with a willing heart, it is not a sacrifice but a gift you give your partner. It is being a caretaker of the spirit of the person you asked to share your life. Studies have repeatedly shown that people who frequently give to others are healthier and happier than those who are typically recipients. In addition, the loving and generous act of giving reinforces the foundation of your relationship.

GIVING TO YOUR PARTNER DOESN'T MEAN GIVING UP YOU

People often feel they will cease to exist as individuals if they really become part of a couple. The result is a knee-jerk opposition to anything that feels as if they are giving in. Compromise feels like surrender, so each person rigidly holds onto their independence and autonomy. They maintain positions at odds with forming a trusting and secure relationship while blaming the other person for inflexibility and control. If one partner makes a reasonable request to have a need met, the other responds as though a frontal assault has been launched and reacts as if their very life is at stake. It becomes a high stakes game of chicken with a win-at-all-costs mentality. The very idea that one's partner has a legitimate position or point of view is inconceivable.

When they first came to my office, Jill and Josh acted like bickering four-year-olds. Whatever one said, the other would immediately contradict. It was a constant barrage of "You did this." "No, I didn't! You did that." I felt I was constantly refereeing a boxing match in which each fighter was hitting below the belt. Josh was hurt and angry because he wanted to take an evening business class that would help him get a promotion. Jill's defense was she was tired after taking care of their three children all day and deserved Josh's help in the evenings. Jill was also upset because Josh was always complaining about how much money she spent. "I work hard at taking care of the house and the kids. Josh makes me feel like a child, having to ask Daddy for permission to buy something nice," Jill complained.

Josh and Jill were engaged in a classic power struggle, with each completely convinced of the "rightness" of their respective positions. The more each focused on what they weren't getting, the more each refused to give the other what they asked for. Each time Josh would ask Jill for one night a week to take this course, she would lash out about how he was trying to control her life and she wasn't going to let him. She would say, "You have responsibilities to the family too. Why do you think it's always my job to take care of the children?" By continuing to lob these grenades at each other, neither was really listening to the legitimate request the other was making. As a result, neither Jill nor Josh was meeting their partner's needs nor getting their own met. The only thing they were accomplishing was increasing the resentment and distance in the relationship.

It is not necessary to lose your identity when you become part of a couple.

Unfortunately, this is a very common approach to relationships. Remember the process of self-betrayal and self-deception? Continuing to do those things you committed to do on your wedding day, and that you know in your heart to be right, will allow you to move past being "right." It is not necessary to lose your identity when you become part of a couple. The way to ensure this doesn't happen is to know who you are and what you are willing to give. People who look to others to fulfill their every desire are bound to be disappointed, laying the groundwork for those ubiquitous "irreconcilable differences." This spells disaster no matter how you look at it. If the couple has children, they end up paying the highest price.

GIVING WHAT MATTERS

Gifts are something we tend to associate with special occasions. But I have a question for you: Is the object in the box all wrapped in shiny paper and ribbon really what your partner has been asking for? What if the gift your loved one wanted most was the fulfillment of the request they have been making for years? Take a moment and think about what would really make your partner happy. Is it spending more time together watching chick flicks or NASCAR? Is it spending less time on the phone with family and/ or friends and more time listening to your partner? Is it finally making plans for that date night you've promised to arrange but never quite got around to? Is it simply a matter of putting your clothes away at the end of the day? Or going to bed at the same time?

The best gifts of all are those we receive on a regular basis. The good morning kiss when your partner comes down to breakfast. The quick response to a request for a change in behavior, like going through the mail or hanging up the wet towels, made to someone we care about. The extra help we get when we are having a rough day. These are the things that fill our hearts and keep us going. So why don't we do these things more often?

Often it's because we don't truly understand how important these "little" things are to our partner. We don't really care about these things ourselves, so they don't register on our radar screens unless our partner specifically mentions them. These are the true gifts we can bestow—gifts that may not show up in the stocking or under the tree, but ones with a much more powerful impact. They can bring lasting change and happiness to our relationships.

FINAL THOUGHTS

Sometimes, we might acknowledge our partner's request and make a promise to do better, but then fall back into our old ways. This may actually make things worse because our partner knows we *can* do what they ask, but we're just not bothering. If we promise and don't follow through, the unintended message we send is that our partner just isn't that important to us. They aren't worth the effort it takes to alter our behavior.

But, if we take our partner's request to heart and really make a concerted effort to honor that need, the payoff is enormous. It is a living illustration of our love for the person we have asked to share our life. It is a genuine demonstration of our ability to put our partner's wants and needs ahead of our own. It isn't necessary to the success of the relationship to *understand* why something is important to our partner. The marvelous gift we can give our partner is fulfilling a request because it will make them feel important and loved. Giving that gift freely will keep our relationship thriving and successful for many years to come.

SUGGESTED DESIGN ACTIVITIES

These questions are designed to get you back in touch with what's important to you *and* to your partner. They are meant to focus your attention on what you know makes both you and your partner feel loved. Making the effort to make your partner feel important and cared about will keep you on track for success.

1. What actions by your partner made you happy when you were dating? What actions of yours made your partner happy?

2. What needs of yours does your partner meet now on a regular basis? What needs of your partner's do you meet?

3. What do you ask your partner for that you aren't getting? What is your partner asking for that you don't give?

4. What keeps you from honoring your partner's requests? What do you think keeps your partner from honoring yours?

5. What would allow you to willingly meet your partner's needs? What do you think would allow your partner to meet yours?

CHAPTER 8
THE TROUBLE WITH ANGELS

Spoil your spouse, not your children.

– Unknown

Statistics show that half of all marriages end before the 25th wedding anniversary. Half of those breakups take place before the eighth anniversary. One common but little acknowledged factor may help explain these statistics. It concerns a group of intruders who are products of the relationship and, most often, are highly desired and anticipated. They are, of course, the children.

These little bundles bring both joy and disruption to the marital relationship. If managed appropriately, the birth of a child can add to the contentment and commitment of the couple. Often, though, the addition of a highly demanding third party can fragment the primary bond between the parents.

MARRIAGE AS THE FOUNDATION FOR THE FAMILY

Michael and Anne have been married for ten years and have two children, Kevin and Jessica. Anne doted on the children as newborns, as many mothers do. But Michael had a hard time relating to his children as infants because they just seemed to "lie there" with a limited ability to interact. And so a parenting pattern developed: Anne became highly involved with the children, while Michael stayed on the sidelines.

The couple's son, Kevin, was almost three when their daughter, Jessica, was born. Because Anne was completely absorbed by her precious baby girl, Michael began to help out more with Kevin. Predictably, as their attention diverged over the children, Anne and Michael began to grow apart. As this distance increased, Anne spent even more time with Jessica, who met her need for love and attention. Michael, meanwhile, began to spend more time with Kevin, who was now more active and involved in athletics like his dad. Anne and Michael can no longer agree on how to raise the children as each has allied with one child instead of with each other. Because of all the time they spend with the children, Anne and Michael don't feel comfortable alone with each other. They have stopped running errands together and neither can remember the last time they went out to dinner. The distance and tension between them now threatens their relationship.

In the above example, Anne and Michael have allowed the children to come between the two of them as partners. Unfortunately, this is a common phenomenon. It is extremely easy to let this happen. Newborns are highly demanding creatures that require a lot of time and attention. In addition, humans have the longest childhood of any mammal. Since research shows that it takes 60 to 90 days for a new behavior to become a habit, it is easy to see how a child-centered focus can become entrenched when we spend several years primarily meeting the needs of our children.

Without a conscious commitment to do otherwise, this natural tendency to concentrate on your children will take a toll on your marriage. Granted, a child-centered focus is not easy to change. Our society encourages it. Countless books and magazine articles promote the idea that if your children are not happy all the time, you are somehow failing as parents. But think about it: if you put your primary focus on the children, you're actually putting the burden on them to hold the family together. This is neither an appropriate job for your children, nor is it one they are capable of accomplishing.

When couples bring a child into their relationship, they must recognize that part of providing for that child is maintaining their own relationship.

When couples bring a child into their relationship, they must recognize that part of providing for that child is maintaining their own relationship. The marital relationship forms the foundation for the family. If you allow that foundation to collapse, your child's world will also fall apart. Just as you wouldn't ignore a problem with the foundation of your house, you and your partner can't afford to ignore issues affecting the foundation of your relationship. You both need to take steps to maintain that foundation even if it means taking focus away from your child at times. It's okay for you and your partner to have a quiet conversation alone in the family room instead of playing your child's favorite game for the umpteenth time. Your child may protest this shift of attention, which may make you waver since we naturally don't want to disappoint our children. What we need to realize, however, is that regularly disappointing our partner puts our children's safety and happiness at greater risk.

ACKNOWLEDGING BIOLOGY

A key challenge children present to the maintenance of the *Us* is the natural tendency for couples to engage in certain survival behaviors. These behaviors help to ensure the continuation of our species. The age-old pattern of male as provider and female as nurturer often emerges with the birth of the first child. This pattern tends to occur regardless of the level of equality in the relationship before the appearance of children.

Sally was pregnant with her fifth child when she and David came to see me for help. David commuted an hour each way to work to be able to afford a house big enough for the family. Sally's main concern was his lack of involvement with the children and limited connection with her. She was also talking about baby number six even though baby five had yet to make its appearance. David admitted that by the time he got home, he frequently had been gone almost 12 hours and was completely exhausted. David was also adamant about one thing. "I love each and every one of my children, but I am not in any way prepared to discuss adding to the family," he proclaimed.

David went on to acknowledge that at the moment of the birth of each of his children he experienced a moment of deep anxiety over how he was going to provide for that additional person. Sally thought that he was being utterly selfish and overly concerned about their financial situation. "I have always believed that love for my children is all that's necessary to see them through whatever life might bring," she firmly stated.

While their respective roles as nurturer and provider may be more pronounced than in most families, Sally and David were nonetheless influenced by biological imperatives to bring the next generation successfully to adulthood and continue the species. Unfortunately, in today's world, unfettered focus on these roles can lead to the destruction of the underlying marital relationship that is the source of stability for that family. As each individual single-mindedly pursues their own role, the distance between partners is likely to grow, with the children becoming their only point of connection. This pattern puts the relationship at risk when the children leave home for lives of their own.

This natural process helps explain the 50% divorce rate by the

25th wedding anniversary. At this point, most children have left home, and if partners are disconnected, they can no longer hide behind their parenting roles. If one partner recognizes this divide before the children leave home but cannot find a way to work through it, a couple may divorce earlier in the relationship. Given the fact that it can take several years for the full effect of children to be felt in a marriage, it is reasonable to propose that the high divorce rate noticeable by year eight—25%—may result from this distancing.

YOUR ROLE AS PARTNER

Finding a healthy balance between your role as partner versus your role as parent is one every couple with children must learn to navigate. What is often not addressed is how harmful not managing those two roles can be to your primary relationship. With all the stresses and pressures experienced on a daily basis, it is all too easy for you and your partner to focus on those things that demand your attention and put off those things that seem to be going okay. Unfortunately for the long-term prospects of your relationship, this lack of attention can be quite harmful.

Creating that necessary balance between your two relationship roles is not easy. Both society and your own instincts encourage you to put the needs of your children first. When asked to name their greatest fear concerning their children, most parents quickly respond that they most fear that their child will be hurt. When asked if they frequently fear their partner being hurt, people often respond with surprise and confusion. It never occurs to many people to equate the two situations. While most of us would never intentionally neglect the needs of one of our children, few of us put the same emphasis on meeting our partner's needs.

When you first become a couple, you pour all of your energy into building that relationship. Your focus is on being together physically, emotionally, socially, and financially. It should come as no surprise that when a child arrives, some of that energy and focus must be transferred to the child. This shift is both reasonable and necessary. The questions we rarely ask are *how much* energy should go to this new relationship and how can a couple come to agreement on this issue? Whatever the verdict, the result is going to be less time together as a couple.

This shift in time and focus requires a big adjustment for both you and your partner. It is crucial to discuss the issue and come to agreement about how your time and energy will be balanced between parenting and partnership. Being together physically, emotionally, and socially now requires attention and planning or it won't happen. And if it doesn't happen, your relationship will be at risk.

Jack and Debbie have been married 16 years and have three children. The level of intimacy in their marriage declined considerably after the birth of their third child, the only boy. One of the main reasons this occurred was because this child, Mark, slept in Jack and Debbie's bed for the first four years of his life. Mark had become a physical barrier Debbie used to keep Jack away. She was very angry with him for spending most of his time with a partner on a business that eventually failed. Debbie felt abandoned and unimportant, especially during the pregnancy. In her resentment, she ended up using Mark as a weapon against her husband.

Debbie's relationships with her daughters weighed in on the parenting side of the relationship equation as well. Her focus on the details of their lives consumed her time and thoughts. She was so wrapped up in their activities, there was no time left over for her and Jack to do anything as a couple. Jack's complaints, if he voiced them at all, were pushed aside as either selfishness or jealousy. But it is not selfish to want to maintain a strong, healthy relationship with the person you chose as your life partner.

Making time to be a couple is necessary for a marriage to not just survive, but thrive. While on the surface it may seem to take away from the family, maintaining a strong *Us* is in the best interests of your children. Studies consistently show that children do best in all aspects of their lives if they live in a stable, two-parent household. Protecting that relationship from all threats is the best gift you can ever give your children.

RELATIONSHIP AS PRIORITY

The way to keep your primary relationship healthy and happy is to put your partner's needs on at least an equal footing with your children's. I realize that this advice goes against common practice, but I believe it is essential to both a satisfying marriage and a happy family. And it's not enough to simply pledge to "pay more attention to my partner." You must take active and intentional steps to promote and protect your marriage.

One way to do this is by dating your partner again. This does not require a large expenditure of money. Setting aside one night a week to enjoy a candlelit dinner or watch a romantic movie after the children are in bed can fit the bill. You can also develop rituals that become part of your daily routine. Decide on a special way to say goodbye to each other in the morning and greet each other at night. Call each other, text, or e-mail at the same time every day. My husband's name is Steve but I haven't called him that, except in public, for years. He is, and will always be, "Esteban." So, if it appeals to both of you, you can create unique names for each other and use them often in everyday conversation. These are small acts of caring, but powerful ones if you practice them regularly. They will help keep you close and connected.

For special occasions such as an anniversary or birthday, put in a bit more planning and effort. You might make arrangements for a night out doing something you both enjoy, or, better yet, a romantic weekend away. Taking time to celebrate these occasions serves as a joyful reminder of why you got together in the first place. If you're celebrating your anniversary, try re-creating your first date or a memorable experience from your honeymoon. Have fun using the traditional anniversary gifts: paper, wood, silver, etc. Don't let it be just another day. On the other hand, you don't have to wait for a special occasion to take a "couple" vacation. Arrange an overnight stay for the children with their grandparents or trade off a night away with good friends. The more time you spend as a couple without the children, the more you protect the romance and intimacy of your marriage.

Another way to protect your connection is to keep your bed to yourselves. As we saw with Jack and Debbie, one place children can intrude on the marriage is in the bedroom. Children do not belong in your bed on a regular basis. They become both physical and emotional barriers to your intimacy and connection. Having a child sleep with you because they are scared or sick may seem harmless at the time. But if it becomes routine, the underlying foundation of your marriage may be damaged. Having your bedroom as a special place where the two of you can escape from the outside world will help with the parent/partner balance. Sharing the marital bed only with each other can deepen the level of intimacy in your relationship.

For some of us, making time to be both a partner and a parent necessitates a fundamental change in how we live. Most of us promised in our marriage vows to forsake all others and cleave only unto each other. The "all others" includes our children. This doesn't mean we neglect our children—not at all. Meeting our parental responsibilities is essential. But it does mean that we must be more intentional in our role as partner. At times, this means putting the needs of your partner ahead of both your own wants and, sometimes, the wants of your children.

Take, for example, a situation brought to me by my clients Sean and Maria. Sean expressed a concern about feeling disconnected from his wife Maria and planned a special dinner and a concert by his favorite band. Their son, Troy, has wanted to see this band but Maria was only mildly interested in going to the concert. Troy begged Maria to let him go in her place and she was tempted to agree. Fortunately, Maria heard Sean's real request. She went home and quietly told Troy, "Not this time. Your dad and I are going to have a good time, just the two of us." Sean overheard this conversation and felt like a priority in Maria's life again.

FINAL THOUGHTS

Putting your marriage first means that you and your partner acknowledge and embrace the foundational concept of the *Us*. It means that the needs of your unit are not only attended to, but honored. It requires that you would no more miss a date with your partner than you would miss one of your children's soccer games or teacher conferences. This transformation in your intention and attention will result in a substantial increase in the happiness and stability of your marriage, and, in turn, the security of your family.

SUGGESTED DESIGN ACTIVITIES

How you and your partner react to your roles as parents will have significant influence on your roles as partners. These questions are designed to help you be intentional in defining those roles, and not leave them subject to chance.

1. How have you seen children affect the marriages of friends and family members?

2. What activities or behaviors did your parents engage in that didn't include their children? Your partner's parents?

3. What concerns do you have about the effect of children on your relationship? What concerns does your partner have?

4. What do you and your partner believe is a mother's role? A father's? How does this fit with your definition of a husband? Your definition of a wife?

5. What rituals, activities, and behaviors do you want to maintain as a couple once you have children? How do you plan on implementing them?

CHAPTER 9
FORSAKING ALL OTHERS

Marriage is our last,
best chance to grow up.

– Joseph Barth, Royal physician

The entire concept of the *Us* is based on the idea that when you get married, you become *you plus*. This means that you remain who you are as an individual, while simultaneously adding the role of partner. The "individual" part of you continues to have roots in two camps that are not directly related to your relationship, but significantly affect it. First, you are still a member of your family of origin—child and/or sibling. These lifelong roles and accompanying behaviors impact the marital relationship and shape what it looks like. The other role you have to learn to manage is that of friend. These two roles alter the partnership dynamic by adding other people into the mix. How these roles are defined and managed by you and your partner will determine the overall functioning and ultimate success of your relationship.

IN-LAW INFLUENCES

David and Janice are having difficulty with his mother over the issue of when they will have children. Patricia, Janice's mother-in-law, is relentless in her pursuit of an immediate grandchild. Whenever the three of them are together, having a grandbaby is all she talks about. Patricia targets Janice specifically because she believes the wife should take the lead in deciding to start a family as soon as possible. Because of this constant pressure, Janice is now reluctant to be anywhere near her mother-in-law. David thinks they should just laugh it off. "Mom just overdoes her enthusiasm," he tells Janice. But she feels that David doesn't understand how hard it is to be pleasant to his mother in the face of her constant harping.

As the holidays draw closer, the couple has started to fight more and more. Janice is resisting getting together with David's family, yet she doesn't know how to avoid it. She is feeling resentful and unsupported. "Whenever I think about spending time with Patricia, I just get anxious. No matter what plan I come up with, I don't see any way around being with her. It's not my idea of a fun time," Janice stated plainly. For his part, David is upset because the holidays are the one time of year he gets to see all of his siblings. As Janice and David sit in chairs on opposite sides of my office, the love they once felt for each other seems as remote as a distant star.

FAMILY OF ORIGIN RESIDUE

Janice and David are experiencing the undue influence of one partner's family of origin. This external pressure can create problems in the marriage that have little to do with how the partners feel about each other. If this pressure is not effectively addressed, it can cause fissures in the relationship that can eventually bring it down. The cause? One partner, in this case David, has not successfully negotiated a change in his role in his family of origin.

As stated earlier, the primary task of committed couples when they become seriously involved is to make the other person of primary importance. This requires you to put the needs of your partner ahead of everyone else in your life. When a family member's interests take precedence over your partner's, the foundation of your relationship can become dangerously stressed. The probability of a breakdown increases if you leave your partner to handle a problem with an interfering member of your own family. Only the individual who is a member of that family can effectively address the issue. Leaving your partner to deal with it is unfair and, ultimately, unworkable. In addition to the external pressure, your partner will feel abandoned and betrayed.

The primary task of committed couples when they become seriously involved is to make the other person of primary importance.

Edward and Amanda came to see me because they had been having frequent arguments. A few months earlier, Amanda's parents had been visiting. During the visit, Edward and his father-in-law, Jim, had a disagreement. Jim kept pushing Edward to watch a television program hosted by a commentator that Edward vehemently disagreed with. Edward felt disrespected in his own home and was quite upset about it. He left the house before he said something that would make matters worse.

Originally, Amanda sided with Edward. But while he was out of the house, her father had a word with her. "A son-in-law should defer to his father-in-law," Jim pronounced. By the time Edward had returned from his effort to calm down, Amanda had switched sides. "You're overreacting," she told him.

Amanda and her family had always been close and got together several times a year. In addition, her father had always run the show. No one, not even Amanda's mother, had ever dared stand up to him. After the blow-up and Edward's refusal to apologize for "stomping out," Jim forbade Edward from attending the high school graduation of Amanda's niece.

Now Edward refuses to spend time in his father-in-law's presence. Amanda, who has always been a daddy's girl, doesn't understand why Edward won't just make peace by apologizing so they can continue to attend the family gatherings. Edward doesn't understand why his wife can't see her father's overbearing behavior for what it is and stand by him. They have been arguing about it ever since.

It can be difficult to take on a family member, especially if it is a parent. But when you get married, you and your partner need to form a new structure with each other at its core. In short, you need to shift your loyalties. How well you and your partner manage this transition and present it to each family will determine how much control you will have over your future. The more dominant the family member is, and the bigger the impact they have on one member of the couple, the more important this establishment and presentation of the *Us* becomes. The sooner you and your partner present yourselves as an independent unit, taking into account the desires of others but honoring your primary commitment to each other, the easier it will be to keep family members at bay.

LEAVING THE NEST

The first test of the cohesiveness of the new *Us* frequently occurs with the first major holiday or celebratory event after the wedding. At that ceremony, most couples have promised to love, honor, and cherish each other, forsaking all others until parted by death. When you are making these promises, it probably doesn't occur to either of you that you're also forsaking Aunt Jenny's famous oyster dressing or Nana's special birthday cake. When autumn rolls around and the leaves start falling, you don't realize that the promises made earlier in the year really meant you were taking an eternal vow to follow your partner's idea of holiday bliss while forsaking your own.

**The first test of the cohesiveness
of the new *Us* frequently occurs
with the first major holiday or
celebratory event after the wedding.**

Trying to negotiate around ingrained traditions is sometimes akin to challenging your partner's politics or religion. But failing to tackle this issue head on can leave your relationship open to problems down the road. Because the issue of family gatherings is so charged with emotion, one of you may be tempted to concede for the sake of peace and harmony. However, if you're not willing to live with this choice for the long term, don't make it now.

Jack and Eleanor have been married for ten years. Thanksgiving has always been a big deal in Eleanor's family because it has served a secondary role as their official family reunion. Each day of the long weekend is scheduled with the precision of a military parade and breaking ranks has not ever occurred to anyone in Eleanor's clan. Jack has dutifully gone along with the program every year since he and Eleanor began dating.

But earlier this year, the couple had their first child, and now Jack wants to stay at home for Thanksgiving and begin a new tradition with just the three of them. He has no objection to joining the family event on Friday, but it's important to him to pass on to his daughter some of the holiday traditions from his side of the family. The pressure (both subtle and not) on Eleanor to maintain her family's tradition is enormous and has resulted in many sharp words and hurt feelings.

Understandably, Eleanor feels caught smack in the middle of both of her families. She is also fighting her own feelings about altering what she's always done for Thanksgiving and assumed she would always do. In addition, until now Eleanor never had to think about what Jack might want because it had never been an issue. Now it *is* an issue—front and center. A holiday she used to think about with warmth and anticipation has now become a source of dread and unhappiness.

The best time to tackle this tricky issue is the very first holiday season you're an established unit, married or not. It's something you should talk about together long before the first leaves begin to change color and the Halloween decorations hit the stores. It's also advisable to take a gradual approach, so that pulling away and establishing new traditions can be done step by step and thereby limit the amount of disruption and hurt feelings that are an almost inevitable part of the process. This measured approach also allows you and your partner to take your time in identifying and implementing what's important to each of you.

Pulling away and establishing new traditions can be done step by step to limit disruption and hurt feelings.

The next step is to introduce these new traditions to your extended families. Start with the ones that will be least disruptive and impact the fewest number of people. This will allow you and your partner to present yourselves as an independent unit without causing major discord. It could be something as simple as staying in a hotel instead of in your old room, or coming to the family homestead Christmas afternoon instead of first thing in the morning. Honoring tradition when you can, but being clear and consistent when you must, will allow others to accept your decisions and allow for changes to occur with minimal "pushback." By starting small, you and your partner will pave the way for more significant changes in the future.

You Want to Keep Doing *What?*

Family holidays are just one of the many landmines a new couple faces as they start down their own road. Another challenge that must be navigated is the role friends play in your new life together. Most of us have some experience with managing existing friendships when we begin to date someone new. Marriage takes this maneuvering to an entirely new level. Your primary alliance is now with your partner, not the best friend you've had since high school. How you choreograph this changing dance will have a major influence on the success of your marriage.

One issue that must be resolved is how much of your old life is incorporated into the new. It is neither necessary nor desirable to cut all ties. If playing sports or going out with friends is important to you, you need to be able to still participate in that activity. How often you engage in these activities may need to change, but dropping them all together does not have to be part of the plan. At the same time, it is essential to modify your old life to accommodate the new responsibilities marriage brings. Your friends need to be supportive of the changes marriage brings.

> **Your primary alliance is now with your partner, not the best friend you've had since high school. How you choreograph this changing dance will have a major influence on the success of your marriage.**

Before Joel got married, he played on two soccer teams and coached two others. He was at practice four nights a week and had games all day on Saturday. After he married Julie, he saw no reason to change his schedule. Julie began to get more and more upset by Joel's absences. She felt she played a distant second to Joel's love affair with soccer. Julie didn't want Joel to stop playing entirely. She just wanted him to spend more time with her. But when he began to miss practices and games in order to have dinner or go to a movie with Julie, Joel's soccer buddies gave him a hard time. Joel felt caught in the middle: he didn't want to let down either his teams or his wife.

When Sheryl was single, she went out at least twice a week with her friends after work. She enjoyed the time she spent with them and being able to be "one of the girls." After marrying Carl, however, she no longer socialized with her girlfriends. But she found herself missing them, and felt as if she had lost something special in her life. Carl encouraged her to call her friends and still go out, but she felt she wasn't being a good wife if she wasn't at home every night. Sheryl was having difficulty deciding what the "right" thing to do was. Her friends weren't making it easier for her because none of them were married and they didn't want her to be a drag on their fun when they were out on the town and flirting with guys.

Both of these couples struggled with negotiating the transition marriage brings. Because they weren't sure what path they should take, their friends didn't know how to behave either. Once each couple determined the parameters of their new lives, their friends fell in line and began to be supportive. Joel and Julie decided he would play on one team and coach another. They also decided that Friday nights and Sunday afternoons would be time set aside for them as a couple. Sheryl determined that meeting for lunch and going shopping or to a movie a couple of times a month with her friends would allow Sheryl to maintain her "girl time" and still feel good in her new role as wife. Carl supported her newfound balance.

It's important for you and your partner to decide what is important to each of you and find a way to incorporate that into your lives. Real friends will be supportive of your decisions, and those that aren't may need to gradually fall by the wayside. In making this decision, it's important to keep your partner's feelings in mind. If you spend most of your free time with your friends or family rather than your partner, they will feel—correctly—like a low priority in your life.

THE PROBLEM WITH FIGHTS

When a married couple has a major argument, friends and family can complicate matters. When a disagreement boils over, our natural tendency is to seek solace and support from family or friends. The problem is that your family and friends are predisposed to take your side. This is the very reason you go to them when you are unhappy. You want to be told you are right and your partner is wrong in this instance. You are looking for that support and feel let down if it is not forthcoming. Unfortunately, when you go outside the relationship for support, it can undermine the relationship itself.

A major problem with bringing family and friends into a fight is that you may change the way that they view your partner. By the very nature of the conversation, your friends and family only hear one side—yours. Your partner is not given the opportunity to share their position. Once you reconcile with your partner, your friends and family won't always understand why you're suddenly happy again with the person you'd so recently been furious with. They may be left with an unpleasant taste in their mouth regarding your partner and your marriage.

It is natural to talk with your friends and family about your relationship. After all, many of them promised to help support your relationship on your wedding day. The key lies in what you tell them and how they respond. How well they know your partner also comes into play. If you have friends who do not know and support you as a couple, they may not be able to provide an objective ear. Single friends may have no point of reference for the normal ebb and flow of feelings that occur in marriage. Divorced friends and family members may have a tendency to tune into the parts of your story that resonate with their own experience. For these reasons, it's important that you tell your friends and family about the positive aspects of your relationship as well as the struggles.

Once again, establishing a strong and healthy *Us* is the best way to prevent undue influence from family and friends. If you and your partner have established the actions you each will take when you're unhappy with the other, the good opinion that others have of your partner and marriage will be maintained. You and your partner need to clearly define who you will talk to and what you will tell them so you can protect your marriage from the biased viewpoints of others in your life. The better you and your partner are about handling disappointments and disagreements on your own, the less need you'll have to complain to outsiders, and the more supportive they can be of your relationship.

FINAL THOUGHTS

Supportive family and friends are crucial to the success of your marriage. However, it is imperative that you and your partner set boundaries for these important people in your life. The primary loyalty must be to your partner, not your family or your friends. You and your partner must define yourselves as a strong *Us* and present that unit to everyone you interact with, no matter how long you have known them or what role they play in your life. It is your job to protect your *Us* at all times, even when you may find your partner challenging. Outsiders will either support your marriage or undermine it. You and your partner are responsible for ensuring that those you interact with on a regular basis support your relationship.

SUGGESTED DESIGN ACTIVITIES

Friends and family are an important and necessary part of our lives. Determining the role they play now you're married is essential for the long term success of your relationship. The following questions are designed to help you and your partner define those necessary boundaries.

1. Do you have any difficulties with your partner's family members or friends? Does your partner have trouble with yours?

2. What boundaries have you established with your family and friends regarding your relationship?

3. What choices have you made in relation to holidays, family celebrations, or family vacations?

4. What choices have you made regarding spending time with your friends without your partner?

5. How have you decided to handle conversations with family and friends when you and your partner are having difficulties?

CHAPTER 10

FOR LOVE AND MONEY

From success you get a lot of things,
but not that great inside thing love brings you.

– Sam Goldwyn, film producer

Money can be a hot-button issue—especially in a marriage. When you were single, you likely spent, saved, and invested on your own, without having to consider the needs or attitudes of another individual. That needs to change. Now, you must find a way to navigate through the challenges of joining your furniture, daily routines, and—yes—finances. You must learn to handle money in ways that respect and strengthen the *Us*. How you and your partner go about handling money can be as distinctive as you want it to be, as long as it works for both of you.

Money brings up all kinds of issues and anxieties that you or your partner may have thought were long buried. Talking about your beliefs about money and sharing financial information is highly personal. This makes it a scary issue because it can highlight behaviors and fears you might prefer your partner not to know. These fears can keep you from an honest exchange of ideas that is necessary to the creation of a strong and durable *Us*. Unfortunately, instead of tackling this difficult issue as a team, many couples get caught up in maintaining a sense of separateness with regards to their finances. Defining income, purchases, or bills in terms of "mine" and "yours" creates both financial and emotional problems for the relationship down the road.

YOUR MONEY STORY

Money is neither good nor bad. It is merely the currency we use to get desired goods and services. So why, then, is it the source of so much tension and distress in a marriage? One of the main reasons is that instead of looking at money as merely a means to an end, we imbue it with a sense of power and allow it to define who we are. Many of life's decisions are determined by how much money we have. It determines the kind of house we live in, the car we drive, the clothes we wear, and how we spend our free time. We use it as a means to measure our self-worth and as a way to define our priorities. The problems arise when you and your partner have different definitions for the meaning money has in your lives.

The meaning you attach to money defines your relationship with it. This relationship, in turn, will affect how you approach financial decisions in your marriage. Money disagreements are one of the two major marital conflicts that lead to divorce. (The other is sex, which will be addressed in a later chapter.) It is critical, therefore, to clarify what role money plays in your lives.

Disagreements involving money arise from multiple sources:

+ How much money does the household have?

+ Who makes more: you or your partner?

+ How are purchasing decisions made?

+ Do you save or spend?

+ How is debt handled?

+ What kind of lifestyle do you want?

The answers to these questions are influenced by your money story. How you and your partner answer these questions will determine how much finances impact your marital happiness.

We tend to look at money and finances from a very personal

perspective. What we have is often viewed as a reflection of who we are, especially in this consumer-driven society. Thus, any discussion you have about your financial circumstances is emotionally laden. When you open the door to that part of yourself, you lay yourself bare. Is it any wonder that money is a source of tension in a marriage? You want your partner to see things your way so you don't have to delve too deeply into your decisions. Having to explain or defend your financial choices leaves you open to the judgment of others. If that person is your spouse, it can create defensiveness and stress in the relationship.

Your relationship with money and how it developed is your money story. It determines your beliefs, values, and habits in terms of earning, saving, and spending money. Once you understand the particular relationship you have with money, you can identify how those beliefs influence your behavior in relation to money. The similarities and differences in how you and your partner view money will determine the role financial issues will play in your relationship.

Samantha's parents divorced when she was eight years old and her mother struggled on her own to make ends meet. Samantha wore hand-me-down clothes from her cousins and was never able to play soccer or go to summer camp. As a result of watching her mother sweat over every bill and count every penny, Samantha decided she wanted to live in a big, impressive house and drive a nice car. She wanted to be able to afford to buy everything she was denied as a child.

When she met her husband David, he made enough money to support that lifestyle. Once married, they bought a sprawling modern home on the shores of a large lake and Samantha drove around in a Lexus suv. Unfortunately, David lost his job as a stockbroker when the market crashed. He was lucky to get a job as an accountant, but they could no longer afford their house on his income alone. To maintain their lifestyle, Samantha had to return to work in public relations. She resents having to work because her money story tells her that it is the husband's job to support the family.

What Samantha is missing is that David *could* support them if her money story didn't also insist that material possessions are a reflection of success and self-worth. Because she has not examined her money story—instead claiming that it's just natural to feel as she does—the resentment building up between her and David threatens to destroy their relationship.

Unless you are very lucky, you and your partner probably have different money stories. One of the challenges of marriage is how to take these different stories and merge them into a new and productive one that works for you both. The only way to do this is to clearly communicate your money story to your partner and vice versa. Unfortunately, this is usually where things go way off course.

MONEY AS A BATTLEGROUND

Our money stories are, by their very nature, personal. Rarely do we have the ability to look at them with an objective, unbiased eye. As a result, we can be very protective and defensive when anyone, especially our partner, tries to challenge our story. It feels as if everything we know is being attacked. We must defend our position to the bitter end, even if it makes no sense to do so.

Often, our knee-jerk response is to attack our partner's money story and beliefs. This provokes a defensive response from them and the initial issue gets lost in the ensuing argument. At this point, it is not unusual for one or both partners to begin using money as a weapon, either tightly controlling it or secretly spending it.

Over the course of my practice I have seen this behavior play out over and over again. Either the partners misunderstand each other's story, or it is so foreign to their way of thinking that it is simply dismissed. For instance, Meredith grew up in a very poor household and has a fear of not having enough money to raise her four children in a stable home. Her husband Andrew has started not one but two businesses over the course of their marriage and he interprets her anxiety as a lack of faith in his ability to be a good provider. The result is that he hides some of his spending and often makes financial decisions without Meredith's input. Andrew's behavior, of course, makes Meredith even more fearful.

Our money stories become part of our world view that is vulnerable to the distortion of self-deception. Andrew believed he was justified in not telling Meredith about his spending habits because she would question them. He was able to frame her fear as unreasonable and irrational, and therefore an infringement on his right to do what he believed to be correct. This belief came to color every discussion they had about money. As a result, they are not working as an *Us* and their marriage is in trouble.

CREATING FINANCIAL GOALS FOR THE *Us*

The approach you take with your partner in defining and implementing your financial goals will influence the overall health of your relationship. The objective in a marriage is to learn how to value each other's relationship with money and develop a way to discuss money and finances from a place of mutual respect. The only way to do this is to first understand how your own money story makes you anxious and reactive. When you are aware of the things that trigger your defensiveness, you will be able to work on controlling those reactions. You will then be more able to discuss those topics with your partner in a calm, rational manner that leads to a resolution, not a fight. If you find that the arguments continue, it is because one or both of you has not made peace with your money story.

Once each of you has identified your own money story, you're ready to create a "mutual money story" that reflects your financial goals as a couple. It is essential to remember there is no right or wrong way to look at money. What is critical is that the two of you create a money story that reflects the experiences, values, and goals both of you have for the future.

Like any other decision in marriage, determining financial goals requires you and your partner to reach an accommodation. This means you both must have input into the discussion in order to create successful buy-in to the proposed solution. The challenge, as always, is to manage your own emotional reaction to the topic of money. You must also identify and adhere to the parameters of your relationship. Some of your parameters include the occupations you and your partner are qualified for, the salaries associated with those occupations, projections for advancement in those occupations, the presence of or desire for children and how you want to raise them, as well as the kind of lifestyle you want to have. It is important that you and your partner examine each of these parameters separately, and then use them as the building blocks for your financial goals. This process may seem a daunting one, but if you take it one step at a time, you will create a workable framework for future financial decisions.

This process came into play relatively early in my marriage. When my husband Steve finished his graduate work, I was about two-thirds done with mine. He was offered a job in another state. My program would not allow me to finish if I moved with him. We decided that, since I could work in my field with the master's degree I had completed, and his career offered greater financial opportunities, we would make the move. We were able to do this because we had a good idea of what we wanted our life to look like. Because it was a mutual decision, an accommodation, it has never been a source of resentment.

Mutual financial goals include, but are not limited to, the following:

+ Where in the country, or world, do you want to live?

+ What size home do you want?

+ Do you want children? How many?

+ Do you both want to work or have one stay home with the children? For how long?

+ What are your priorities for spending money?

+ What are your priorities for saving money?

+ When do you want to retire?

+ What is an acceptable debt level?

+ How do you prepare for the unexpected events of life?

+ What balance do you want between living in today and planning for tomorrow?

The answers you and your partner define will both reflect and determine your financial goals.

MONEY MANAGEMENT FOR YOUR US

Another issue that arises frequently between couples is control over their finances. Who will pay the bills and when will they get paid? Who will be in charge of the checkbook? Who makes the rules for making purchases, large or small? Many of the disagreements I see over money result from one partner being in the dark about how much money there is and how it is being spent.

Jennifer and Dan constantly fought over money. He wielded

absolute control over their finances and would get very upset if she spent more than he thought was necessary. Jennifer was angry because she felt he treated her like a child. She knew how much money they made, and even though she didn't pay the bills, she knew they were financially okay. Jennifer thought it was unfair for Dan to make her account for every penny she spent. After one particularly bad fight, Jennifer convinced Dan to walk her through the monthly statements. Once he allowed her access to both the income and expenses, she was able to see exactly where the money went and when during the month bills had to be paid. Jennifer was then able to see Dan's financial plan and began making purchasing decisions more in line with the goals Dan developed. Keeping her out of the loop had the exact opposite effect of the one he wanted.

Like Jennifer, not knowing the particulars about your finances can lead to challenges in your relationship. Not having the relevant facts can lead to misunderstandings about your partner's actions or motives. It can also lead to decisions and behaviors based on incomplete information. You and your partner need to develop a plan that ensures that both of you know how much money you have and how you are spending it. The first part of the plan should be the discussion of the financial goals of your *Us*. Everything you and your partner do from then on should be in support of those mutually agreed-upon goals. In addition, both of you must have an active role in the ongoing management of your finances. This can take one of several forms:

+ You pay the bills while your partner balances the checkbook.

+ You and your partner create a budget and you examine your spending against that budget when you balance the checkbook.

- One of you takes responsibility for the bills and check-book, but you have a quarterly meeting to examine the books together.

Another question you and your partner must resolve is how money should be spent. Again, this should flow from the financial goals the two of you have agreed to. In determining the guidelines for spending, you and your partner will need to address individual priorities in a way that supports your common goals. Again, the guidelines you create are completely up to you, but both of you have to be on board. The following are some common ways of addressing spending decisions:

- You and your partner decide together on every spending decision.

- Each month, you and your partner set a dollar amount that can be spent, and any spending over that amount must be mutually agreed upon.

- Each of you is responsible for spending related to particular categories, such as automotive, food, utilities, etc.

- You and your partner define what constitutes major purchases and mutually agree to those purchases.

In whatever way you and your partner decide to handle your finances, it is vital you both have a clear understanding of what is happening with your money. It is also imperative that you and your partner reach a genuine accommodation about your finances. Making concessions on this essential issue breeds resentment and distrust, which will undermine a healthy, successful marriage.

OPTIONS FOR EVERYDAY FINANCES

There are as many ways to handle finances as there are couples. These options range from keeping your financial lives completely separate to both of you embracing the concept of "our money." The following are some examples of the methods of money management couples adopt to deal with regular life expenses.

JOINT CHECKING ACCOUNT: This is an account where both partners are listed as "owners" of the account. Either individual may write checks against the balance. In this method, all money received by either spouse is deposited into this one account and all expenses are paid from it.

SEPARATE ACCOUNTS: Each individual has their account that can be accessed only by that person. The individual places all money they receive into this account and pays those expenses previously agreed to. In this system, there is no co-mingling of money. It is strictly his and hers.

SEPARATE AND JOINT ACCOUNTS: A joint account is used to pay common expenses such as housing, utilities, and food. Each party deposits an agreed-upon amount each month to cover the bills. This could be either a percentage of salary or a specific dollar amount. The rest of the money received is kept in separate, individual accounts to be used at the discretion of the owner.

JOINT CHECKING WITH ALLOWANCE: Most of the funds are deposited in a joint checking account to which both parties have access. In addition, an identified amount of money is allotted to each partner on a regular basis to spend or save, as they desire.

A couple may start out using a more separate approach and

move toward a more joint approach over time. This often occurs if a couple moves in together before marriage. It also can arise if one partner has had financial difficulties in the past, especially if they have a bad credit history and/or continuing responsibility for outstanding debt. Until these issues are resolved, they can create "financial distance" and growing tension in the relationship.

Wendy and Tom were planning to marry and decided that the cost of maintaining two households was an unnecessary expense. Tom made more money than Wendy did, and though they chose their new house together, he purchased it. They used the separate checking account method of handling their bills.

But Wendy felt like an unequal partner in this arrangement. While she contributed less money overall to the household, she actually paid more in terms of the percentage of her income. Nonetheless, Tom tended to have the upper hand in their discussions over what to buy and when to buy it. Wendy had already begun to monitor her requests to purchase any item that was not an absolute necessity. She was concerned about how this established pattern of decision-making inequity would affect their marriage.

Even though Wendy was nervous about broaching the subject of money with Tom, she knew if they didn't resolve this financial issue soon, it could affect her decision to marry him. To her surprise, Tom was very open to revisiting how money would be handled after they married. Once he understood Wendy's concerns, Tom immediately made arrangements to put her name on the deed. They also decided to open a joint checking account where all their money would be pooled as soon as they were married.

FINAL THOUGHTS

Developing and implementing the *Us* will keep fights over money at bay because you will have identified yourself as a team. Defining mutual financial goals and consistently engaging in behaviors that support those goals is what will keep money from being an impediment to a successful and enduring relationship. You and your partner need to be able to communicate openly and honestly about finances, avoid keeping money secrets, and regularly assess your goals and the progress you are making in meeting those goals. You will need to learn to manage your own anxieties and long-held beliefs about money and stay focused on the new money story you and your partner have chosen to create. Deciding together how money is earned, spent, and saved, and then following that plan, will strengthen the foundation of your marriage.

SUGGESTED DESIGN ACTIVITIES

These questions are designed to help you and your partner understand your relationship with money. Defining the role money and finances will play in your marriage will keep disagreements to a minimum. This will help you and your partner manage one of the most common stressors in marriage.

1. What are your beliefs about money? What are your partner's beliefs? What is your money story? What is your partner's?

2. What difficulties do you have in addressing money issues with your partner? What difficulties does your partner have?

3. What are the money goals for your *Us*?

4. Do you know where the money goes? Does your partner know? What rules do you and your partner want to make for managing finances?

5. How have you and your partner decided to handle money in your relationship, both day-to-day and over the long term?

CHAPTER 11

SAY WHAT YOU MEAN; MEAN WHAT YOU SAY

Well-timed silence hath more eloquence than speech.

– Martin Farquhar Tupper, writer & poet

The two most frequent complaints I hear from my clients are, "We don't communicate anymore," and "I love my partner, but I'm just not *in* love anymore." What they don't realize is that these statements can be just two ways of saying the same thing. It's impossible to feel connected to someone when you think they don't listen to you or respect what you're saying. When you aren't connected to your partner, it becomes very difficult to have a truly intimate relationship. If you feel distant from your partner, you'll need to identify what's missing from your communication process and bring it back into the partnership. This single action can dramatically improve your chances of enjoying a long and successful marriage.

John Gray says men are from Mars and women are from Venus. I'm not sure we're from different planets, but I do think we may be two different species—at least psychologically. Nowhere is this more apparent than in the areas of communication and intimacy. On average, women use 7,000 more words a day than men. Not only do we use more words, but the number of neurons in our corpus collosum (the part of the brain that connects the two hemispheres) is greater in women. Some women might take this to mean that they communicate better than men do. After all, most women have absolutely no problem being understood by their female friends. Therefore, they conclude, men must be the source of error when there is a communication issue.

What is often overlooked is the reality that women and men communicate differently. The intent of the conversation, the tone, and the meaning we give to words play large roles in the effectiveness of our communication. In these areas, men and women often make different assumptions and have different goals. We'll come back to this shortly.

> **What is often overlooked is the reality that women and men communicate differently.**

One of the challenges of working with couples is finding a way to get at the individual pain lying beneath the problems each partner presents. This requires the ability to bridge the gap between what is said and what is felt. It is during this process that a couple's style of communication is exposed. This pattern of communication is a function of the man's individual style, the woman's individual style, *and* their way of responding to each other. Changing any one of these three patterns will result in a new and, hopefully, more effective manner of communication.

GENDER DIFFERENCES IN COMMUNICATION

The first step in changing a pattern of marital communication is to identify your and your partner's communication style. This identification begins with the general differences in the ways men and women communicate. Men tend to take a more direct approach in getting to the heart of the matter. They then want to "fix" it and move on. Women, on the other hand, frequently take a softer approach and phrase wants or needs in the form of requests. They often want to make sure all angles have been considered so no one feels left out or hurt.

Gender differences in processing verbal information also come into play during a discussion. My male clients frequently report feeling outgunned during a conversation with a woman. Their partners fire questions and statements at them so quickly that they tend to become lost or overwhelmed. When they try to retreat to gather their thoughts, their partners advance with more words and feelings. It's at this point in a discussion that many men give in just to escape further interaction. But often, their resentment builds over not being given the time to gather their thoughts and present their case.

In therapy, this pattern of interaction is known as Pursuer-Distancer. One partner, usually the woman, pushes hard for inter-action. The other partner, usually the man, tries to break away to assimilate all the information he's been given. This perceived retreat makes The Pursuer feel shut out, so she pushes all the harder. At this point, The Distancer learns that it is not in his best interest to participate in conversations with his partner, and he increasingly keeps his thoughts and feelings to himself. This pattern continues to build, along with its accompanying resent-ments and frustrations, until nearly every conversation escalates into an argument. The woman blames the man for not being able to communicate; the man blames the woman for talking too much and pushing too hard.

CONFLICT AVOIDANCE

Another frequent pattern of communication between partners is "conflict avoidance." While I have met very few people who deliberately seek out conflict, I do know many who actively avoid it. Most of these people grew up in homes where they either never experienced conflict, so it scares them, or it was so much a part of their early lives that they never want to encounter it again.

These individuals have learned that expressing their thoughts and feelings is either uncomfortable or actually dangerous. It's hard to get them to express an opinion, let alone request that one of their needs be met. They communicate by addressing an issue indirectly, using inference or example. When faced with another's wish or demand, they frequently give in even if it isn't what they really want. Their behavior suggests that their viewpoint or feelings aren't as valid as those of others—and certainly not worth creating a disturbance over. When this pattern is present, trying to resolve an issue is like trying to catch a fish barehanded—you expend a lot of effort but usually end up with nothing.

One of the most common problems in a marriage occurs when one person becomes dissatisfied with the relationship and cannot find a way to resolve the underlying issue. I frequently hear that one partner has given up trying because it causes too much conflict with the other partner. It's just easier to stay quiet and maintain the status quo. The main problem with this tactic is that the concern doesn't go away. It just goes underground.

The status quo does change. It starts, however, as an internal change that eventually seeps out into a person's behavior. It is like the Steve McQueen movie, *The Blob,* when the people lock themselves in the movie theater to escape the terrifying thing that absorbs everyone in its path. The Blob finds its way into the theater by oozing under the doors and through the air vents and tries to engulf the people anyway. In a similar way, your emotions will find their way out. It is not a direct and upfront approach but one that is more muddled and often backhanded. The conflict is still there but remains unresolved because it has become so elusive.

AVOIDANCE FOR NOW

Charlie and Alice have been married for ten years. Alice has a 15-year-old daughter and the couple has a three-year-old son. What brought them to my office was the state of their finances, issues with Alice's daughter, and an inappropriate relationship Charlie had on the Internet. Alice is frustrated because the only time they seem to deal with these problems is when she forces the issue. Charlie gets defensive and argumentative, which leads to Alice losing her temper. The fight escalates until one of them leaves the house. The subject is dropped until the next time Alice gets frustrated.

Both Alice and Charlie report that they get along pretty well between these fights. When I ask why they don't pick a time to address the issue when they both are calm and can have a rational discussion, they state that they want to avoid a conflict when things are going okay. Both admit they are still bothered by the problems even when not actively addressing them. They also state that the period between fights is getting shorter and shorter. Both seemed surprised when I point out that they really aren't successfully avoiding the conflict at all. They are just avoiding the conflict "for now."

Charlie and Alice are like people who put off going to the doctor because they're afraid the doctor is going to say something is wrong with them. That approach simply postpones treatment until the problem becomes so serious that drastic measures are required. If the condition is left unattended for too long it may become untreatable. Avoiding conflict frequently has the same result. I have yet to meet anyone who really *enjoys* dealing with conflict within a relationship. What I do know is that couples who face their issues head-on have a much greater chance of success than couples who put their heads in the sand and hope their differences will magically go away.

While disagreements in a relationship are inevitable, conflict is a choice. Conflict occurs when both of you view your position as the only valid one and try to get your partner to see it "your way." It's about not wanting to see your partner's viewpoint because that might involve having to move out of your comfort zone and do something different. The alternative is to avoid the issue and hope to outlast your partner's desire for change. If the issue really is unimportant, this tactic may work. Unfortunately, if the concern is serious, avoiding the process of resolution can be fatal to the relationship.

The trouble is, addressing a "hot button" issue might be very difficult for one partner. It seems that no matter how small the issue or how calmly it is broached, the resulting conversation escalates into a fight. Most often this occurs because one of you moves from a specific complaint to a more global criticism. Charlie does this when he notices Alice's daughter not taking her dishes from the table to the sink and exclaims, "Your daughter never does anything around the house." Once this happens, the immediate response is for the partner who feels attacked to become defensive. At that point, any further effort to reach resolution is futile.

COMPLAINTS, CRITICISM, AND CONTEMPT

Dr. John Gottman, a world renowned psychologist, followed 2,000 married couples for over two decades. He was able to predict with 94% accuracy which couples would separate within four years. In his book *Why Marriages Succeed or Fail,* Gottman identified complaint, criticism, and contempt as key to the long-term outcome for a relationship. His definitions are as follows:

+ **COMPLAINT** is a specific statement of anger, displeasure, distress, or other negativity. For example: "We don't go out as much as we used to and I miss that."

✦ **CRITICISM** is much less specific. It is more global and may contain an element of blame. For example: "You never take me anywhere."

✦ **CONTEMPT**, like criticism, is global but it includes the intent to insult and psychologically abuse one's partner. Some of the signs of contempt are:

Name-calling: Using insults such as stupid, ugly, fat, or jerk.

Hostile humor: Using comic relief to thinly disguise put-downs.

Mockery: Ridiculing or making fun of another's words or actions.

Body language: Sneering, rolling the eyes, or curling the lip.

The pathway from complaint, through criticism, to contempt is fairly straightforward. It's also a pathway that is relatively easy to start down. No one likes to be told that one of their behaviors is irritating or disagreeable. Most likely, your first reaction will be to defend the action or minimize its effect. But if you minimize or dismiss the complaint, your partner will feel unheard or, worse, uncared for. If you make a promise to change the behavior but don't follow through, again you're sending the message to your partner that their feelings don't matter. This is the point where criticism enters the relationship.

A HEALTHY PATHWAY FOR MARRIAGE

When you have to repeat a request over and over again, you begin to over-focus on what is wrong with the relationship. I am currently working with a couple on the brink of divorce over the husband's refusal to address his wife's complaints over the years. "I just want the house to be picked up. I'm not asking for it to be spotless, just not so cluttered. I work a full-time job and have asked for Phillip's help to keep things under control," Marsha complained. "The papers lying around don't really bother me," he responded. Phillip hasn't recognized the importance of Marsha's requests because they aren't things that matter to him. Marsha's thinking is that if she has to do it all herself, she might as well be alone. This global focus on the negative has allowed her to be blinded to what is working in the relationship and what has kept them together. She overlooks how much fun they have together traveling, as well as how much Phillip helps out with their four boys. Fortunately, contempt has not yet entered the picture, but Marsha's level of frustration is palpable.

When your partner comes forward with an issue or concern about your relationship, you need to make a real effort to consider your partner's position seriously.

The key to staying off the criticism pathway is simple but not easy. It requires you both to put the needs of the relationship ahead of your own individual needs. Your partner's needs and desires should become important to you because they are important to your partner. It doesn't matter whether you have similar needs and desires—the point is, your partner has them. When your partner comes forward with an issue or concern about your relationship, you need to make a real effort to consider your partner's position seriously. This doesn't mean you ignore your own feelings or concerns, just that you recognize your partner may see things from a different perspective. When you both are able to do this for each other, the overall view of the relationship remains positive and complaints are dealt with before they morph into criticism. There are tools and techniques couples can learn to be able to address issues at the complaint level. These will be introduced to you later in the chapter.

COMPONENTS OF COMMUNICATION

One of the major complaints I hear from couples is that they have trouble communicating. I listen to their concerns and provide my interpretation about what is really going on. After some discussion, couples will often accept the new interpretation. Inevitably, one of the partners, usually the woman, will then state, "I have been saying that for years." She expresses both relief that the issue has been identified and frustration that it's taken a veritable stranger to get her partner to acknowledge the source of the tension she identified a long time ago.

What may appear on the surface as a simple consensus between partners about the root of the seemingly unsolvable problem is actually a dramatic shift in the pattern of communication that had developed over the life of the issue. Until this point, there had been a lot more going on in relation to the problem than either partner could acknowledge. Vested interest in one's position, unstated expectations or assumptions, and early life experiences are just some of the underlying influences at play. Developing and applying better communication techniques allows couples to make these pattern shifts on their own.

Deborah Tannen discusses the many levels of communication in her book *I Only Say This Because I Love You*. Research has shown that less than 10% of communication involves actual words. The rest is determined by tone of voice, facial expression, body language, emotional reactivity, and one's past experiences with the other person. Usually communication about a contentious issue has a tumultuous emotional history that continues to bubble beneath the surface and obstructs the ability to find a resolution.

In revisiting the same issue over and over again, we tend to become more limited in our viewpoint and understanding of the matter at hand. In other words, most of us take a stand that becomes more a matter of personal pride than rationality.

When you and your partner reach an impasse on an issue, it is advisable to go back to the beginning and start again. First, you need to clearly identify what the real issue is. This will require some excavation of all the junk that has accumulated around the problem over time. It is quite likely that the person who first identified the problem was either unclear about the actual dilemma or uncertain about the desired outcome. For example, I hear time and again in my office that one partner wants the other partner to listen. It often becomes clear what they really want is for their partner to *agree* with them. Those are two very different outcomes which, when confused, lead to misunderstandings and resentments. For good communication, it is essential to be clear about both the nature of the problem and the desired outcome.

**First, you need to clearly identify
what the real issue is.**

A second issue that affects the quality of communication is the degree of emotional "charge" accompanying the issue at hand. Communication is, by definition, an exchange of information about a particular topic. When emotional attachment to a subject is high, the ability to exchange information decreases. What often occurs is not communication but lecture, demand, or plea. Information travels in one direction only.

The consequence of this unilateral presentation is often bitterness and defiance on the part of the receiving party. Once this occurs, resolution of the problem becomes impossible. Therefore, it is crucial to limit the emotional intensity surrounding the problem under discussion. In my office, I help clients learn how to communicate more calmly and, therefore, more effectively. They learn to acknowledge their emotional reaction, and to manage those emotions and choose a more focused, productive response.

A third component of good communication is to clarify the level of the conversation you and your partner are having. These levels are a function of the depth of the conversation, which ranges from superficial to complex. If you and your partner are conversing at different levels, you are not having the same conversation. The three levels of communication are:

+ **EVENT:** This is the most superficial level and involves a simple action, such as paying a household bill or letting your partner know when you will be home for dinner.

+ **TOPIC:** This conversation takes place at a more global level and involves the larger concept of how the rent or mortgage fits into your budget, or whether having dinner together is important to you.

+ **ISSUE:** This is the deepest level of conversation and involves your core values and beliefs. It touches on what money means to you or the wish to feel important to your partner.

If your partner is looking at the situation at the event level and you are considering it at the topic or issue level, you are not having the same conversation. One way to recognize a mismatch is if you keep having the same conversation over and over again. One of you may think you have reached agreement, but the next time the mortgage is due or you miss dinner, you find yourself dragged back into the same old conversation. Another way to know you are at different levels is if one of you seems to have an overreaction to what the other feels is a simple observation or comment. This is why it's so important for you and your partner to clarify the conversation you're really having. It is only when you are sure you're on the same level that you can begin to resolve your concerns.

TOOLS FOR CHANGE

When asked about key components of communication, most people immediately mention effective speaking and listening. There is, however, one other aspect of communication you need to take into account when you and your partner tackle a challenging concern. This third critical factor in communication is timing. Choosing *when* you have a conversation is as important as what you talk about. Because timing is so essential—and often ignored—we will address it first.

Choosing *when* you have a conversation is as important as what you talk about.

TIMING: Most conversations that involve troubling issues between partners occur without planning or forethought. One of you gets upset about something. The upset person usually does one of two things: addresses the issue immediately or stews about it for a while and then brings it up, seemingly out of the blue.

Each of these options carries hazards. If you respond immediately, you'll probably start off emotionally agitated. As a result, the discussion will most likely degenerate into mutual criticism and anger. On the other hand, if you stew a while, you'll likely spend time writing the script of the discussion according to your agenda. If you've waited and plotted your side of the conversation and then launch the debate without warning, your partner will feel ambushed and most likely react defensively. Either response will make it impossible to productively resolve the issue.

The most effective way to approach a difficult conversation is to time it well—for both of you. Find a time when you both have plenty of time to talk and when interruptions are not likely to happen. Prior to the conversation, make certain that the topic of discussion is clear to both of you. Each of you must have time to fully understand what is to be discussed so you can think through your position. That way, neither of you will feel at a disadvantage.

It's also important to agree to break off the conversation as soon as one of you gets upset. By "upset" I mean an emotional reaction so strong that you can no longer manage your responses. Once this level of emotion enters the picture, your ability to listen to your partner and to comprehend their position becomes very difficult. It doesn't mean you can't cry or have hurt feelings. It does mean that if one of you becomes uncontrollably angry or hysterical, you need to take a break. Very few matters need to be resolved immediately. Remember, it's in the best interest of your relationship to take your time to develop an *effective* solution, not just a quick one.

Several of my clients have objected to the concept of taking a time-out when the conversation starts to spin out of control. They fear that once interrupted, the conversation will be dropped and the topic not addressed until the instigator gets upset and brings it up again. You can keep this from happening by agreeing to a specific time to revisit the topic. This can be in five minutes, an hour later, or the next day. The purpose of this time-out is to get emotions under control, not to avoid having the conversation. Once the conversation is rescheduled, both partners have time to process what has been said and to revisit their position.

Choosing the right time for a critical conversation is a first positive step. Let's now turn to speaking and listening as other key elements of effective communication.

SPEAKING: Most people think they don't need any help in getting their point across. They know what needs to be said and they are intent on saying it. To be an effective speaker, however, it is important to:

+ Keep the conversation on topic and avoid straying to unrelated matters.

+ Limit your comments to your own thoughts and feelings on the subject—don't invite your partner's defensiveness by interpreting their behavior and emotions.

+ Do not use the word "you." In this context, "you" becomes a fighting word. It gets your partner riled up and makes it almost impossible for them to hear a legitimate request for behavior change. This may require grammatical gymnastics but it will result in a successful outcome.

+ Make a conscious effort to avoid using "never" and "always"—these all-or-nothing words encourage contradiction and denial and divert your partner's attention from your point.

If you approach the situation calmly and take responsibility for your own feelings and behavior, you increase the likelihood of a positive outcome for your discussion.

LISTENING: Almost everyone agrees that listening is essential to a conversation. It is, however, the component of communication that presents the most difficulty for most of us. We believe we understand the situation at hand and know what's right. We are certain that if our partner would just listen to us and do it our way, the problem would be resolved. Unfortunately, our partner believes exactly the same thing.

Being a good listener requires that you suspend your own ideas for a moment and concentrate openly and completely on your partner's position. A well-known and effective technique for ensuring that you understand your partner's position is "reflective listening." In this approach, you paraphrase or reflect back what you hear your partner saying. This allows for any misunderstandings to be clarified before an inappropriate response is given.

Reflecting back your partner's statements or feelings doesn't necessarily mean you agree with your partner. It simply means that you understand their position. It also slows down the conversation in a positive manner and allows both of you to keep your emotions under control. It is very important not to presume that you know what your partner is thinking or feeling. Don't feel compelled to finish sentences or provide other assistance to your partner if they take a moment to compose their thoughts. The silence may be uncomfortable, but it is necessary to give your partner time to consider their words or position. These lulls are essential to the listening component of productive conversations.

Final Thoughts

To maximize the chance of communicating well with your partner:

+ Choose an appropriate time to discuss a difficult topic,

+ Get clear about what the topic is,

+ Take ownership of your own thoughts and feelings, and

+ Take the time to really listen to your partner instead of preparing your response.

If you practice these communication skills, you will find that resolving differences will be far easier than if you rely on your old conversational habits.

SUGGESTED DESIGN ACTIVITIES

Effective communication is key to a successful relationship. Now might be a good time to examine how you and your partner communicate. Finding answers to the following questions will help you both learn to have productive conversations.

1. How do you approach difficult topics with your partner? How does your partner approach you?

2. How do you manage your emotions during difficult conversations? How does your partner manage theirs?

3. What conversations do you and your partner have repeatedly? What conversational level do you think you're on? What level is your partner on?

4. What keeps you from truly hearing your partner's position? What gets in your partner's way of hearing yours?

5. What specific steps can you and your partner take to have more productive conversations?

CHAPTER 12

THE IMPORTANCE OF REAL INTIMACY

*Love at first sight is easy to understand,
it's when two people have been
looking at each other for a
lifetime that it becomes a miracle.*

– Amy Bloom, writer & therapist

Intimacy is one of the fundamental features of marriage. Webster's New Collegiate Dictionary defines intimacy as "a state marked by very close association, contact or familiarity; a state marked by a warm friendship developing through long association; and a state of a very personal or private nature." Many people, especially couples, equate intimacy with sex. In truth, it is so much more than that.

Intimacy is both a function of the health of a relationship and one of its most rewarding elements. When things are going well, intimacy seems to occur easily and often. Likewise, one of the first warning signs of problems in a relationship is a decrease in affection and closeness. I'm not talking about the ebbing of hot passion. This transpires naturally over the course of a long-term relationship. I mean the decline of casual touching, use of pet names, exchange of secret looks, and other signs of long-held affection.

Sam and Erin mentioned two wonderful weekends they'd enjoyed just before one of their sessions with me. They then expressed concern that they couldn't seem to maintain that level of closeness all the time. These weekends were not romantic getaways—simply visits to each of their families. The couple seemed confused—their physical intimacy had not increased during these trips. But the tension between them was noticeably lower than when they were at home.

When I asked Sam and Erin how they'd spent their time during those weekends, they said they'd spent a lot of time together in the car and participated in enjoyable activities, such as hiking, just the two of them. I pointed out that on these trips, they had been able to focus on each other and simply be in the moment together. When we examined how they spend their time at home, they realized they tended to focus a lot on issues and activities outside the relationship, such as work, social networking, and their individual hobbies. I suggested that they find ways to connect each day—just the two of them—to keep the intimacy they enjoyed on their trips present in their daily lives.

As my clients discovered, how they interact with each other on an ordinary day determines how connected they feel. This elusive but very real connection is one and the same as intimacy. It's what allows us to share our thoughts, feelings, hopes, and dreams with those we love. In order to be intimate, we must be able to be vulnerable. In order to be vulnerable, we must feel safe. This feeling of safety is established by how we are treated in the relationship.

Intimacy requires the ability to be open and honest with yourself and your partner. Anything that stifles that openness diminishes how close your relationship can be. The level of intimacy you experience can serve as a barometer to the health of your marriage.

If you feel separate and apart from your partner, it's like a fever signaling an illness. I've mentioned this before but it's worth repeating: making sure that you are connected with your partner each and every day is essential to the long-term health and happiness of your relationship.

CHERISHING YOUR PARTNER

I link intimacy to a vow most of us make on our wedding day: the promise to cherish our partner. Most of us take seriously and mean to fulfill the marital pledge to love, honor, and cherish each other until "death do us part." Most of us have a pretty good understanding of love and honor. The concept of cherishing our partner, however, often gets lost in the stresses and pressures of daily life.

When you cherish your partner, you demonstrate every day that you care for them and are glad to have them in your life. You make every effort to meet your partner's needs. Each morning you ask yourself, "How will I make my partner feel loved today?" You regularly evaluate your performance in the relationship from your partner's viewpoint. If your partner feels cherished, they will be a responsive, loving mate. And isn't that what you want from your relationship?

Cherishing your partner means that you willingly do things for them for no other reason than for the happiness it will bring. Do you remember my client who said that if he did what his wife wanted, she would win? This is a mistake on several levels. First, it told me he and his wife were competing, not working as a team, which we discussed in a previous chapter. It also revealed that the level of intimacy in the marriage was wanting. Because he was looking at the relationship as a struggle between his desires against hers, the effect was one of separate focus. This separateness led to frustration, anxiety, and discord. When these destructive characteristics are present, intimacy cannot flourish.

INTENTIONAL INTIMACY

When you first fell in love with your partner, you probably spent hours trying to figure out what would make them happy and want to be with you. You listened for hints about things your partner enjoyed—the kind of music, the type of activities, favorite restaurants, etc. Undoubtedly, you felt thrilled when you surprised your partner with just the right gift or experience. The pleasure you received from making your partner happy was all the reward you needed. These special moments brought you closer and helped move your relationship to the next level. You laid the groundwork for further intimacy.

If you want to reignite that flame, you must once again act with intention. Do you know your partner's likes and dislikes? What would your partner enjoy doing most on your next vacation? Do you listen to your partner for subtle clues as to what they might want as a present? When was the last time you planned a special night out just for the two of you? How do you leave each other in the morning? How do you come back together at the end of the day? Do you have special names for each other or special activities you do only with each other?

When you establish rituals that serve to connect you and your partner, you open the door to intimacy. When you make your partner feel special and important, intimacy embeds itself in the relationship. The key to ensuring that intimacy remains ever present in your relationship is by intentionally acting in ways that make your partner feel cherished every day.

MEN, WOMEN, AND INTIMACY

Acting with intention in relation to intimacy is a good start to strengthening the level and quality of your relationship. But what couples tend to focus on most is how to stay connected physically. When I first began working with couples on this issue, I thought the design of the human sexual/emotional system was haywire. Men often need physical intimacy in order to connect emotionally. Most women, however, need to feel an emotional connection to be able to respond on a physical level. After a while, I discovered that when everything is in its proper place, the system works perfectly. By this I mean that both partners have to be willing to give to each other in order to make the union complete. To make this happen, it is necessary to understand the inherent differences between men and women and why these differences exist.

Despite all of the advances we've made to try to eliminate societal differences between men and women, the biological differences that ensure the survival of the species remain. In order to appreciate these differences, we must examine why they exist. Looking at the issue from an evolutionary standpoint it would appear that we are not very far removed from our cave-dwelling ancestors. Because life then was often short and brutal, it was vital for the species to increase its population at every opportunity. The way men and women approach physical intimacy today is a direct result of this ancient need to produce many offspring and raise as many of these children to adulthood as possible. Then, as now, men and women play different, complementary roles in the partner-choosing process.

Men fall in love with their eyes. They are biologically hard-wired to gravitate toward women who are young and healthy in order to increase their chance of reproducing. They are also wired to be ready to procreate at a moment's notice. The time it takes for a man to identify an opportunity for physical intimacy, become ready for it, and complete the task is about 15 minutes on average.

But this natural tendency for men to get down to business doesn't always work well in a committed, long-term relationship. It takes time and attention to the needs of one's partner to make a relationship work. Man's evolutionary penchant to prowl and hunt can complicate this process. It isn't that men aren't interested in intimacy and connection in a relationship; it's just that they express it differently. Sex is the language men use to express their desire for intimacy. How willing a man is to be emotionally open—not just physically available—will influence how connected he can be to his partner for the long term.

Women, on the other hand, fall in love with their ears. Their mental development involves a greater use of, and dependence on, words. Women are biologically hard-wired to pay attention to the larger perspective and the context of a situation. They take in the entirety of their surroundings, make the necessary connections, and then pay no more attention to what doesn't matter. These abilities are necessary in order to be able to recognize and act on potential threats to their children. It is also part of the reason women take longer to become aroused physically. Physiologically, women are just starting to relax and give in to sexual urges when men are finishing up. This timing mismatch may seem to be a set-up for frustration but it's actually a way for a woman to identify a mate who is able to control himself and allow her to catch up to him. This ability often reflects a man's maturity and stability, and therefore his capacity to be a good partner and father for the long term.

In important ways, 21st century couples behave much the same as their early ancestors. Even though humans have long since moved into safer environments and tamed many of the threats that once resulted in early death, our biological systems have not caught up. When it comes to physical intimacy, the old biological urges rule. Men frequently want to get right down to business. Women, however, need to move more slowly and deliberately.

When couples behave only in accordance with their hard-wired sexual instincts, the result is often only physical contact rather than true connection. While there is nothing wrong with this type of contact, it will not result in real intimacy. When the behavior is driven by natural urges as opposed to genuine caring, the focus often is on fulfilling one's own needs without concern for one's partner.

In order to create true intimacy on a physical level, you must temper your own level of desire with attention to the needs of your partner. This focus on the other person allows you to reveal your true feelings. Each of you makes a conscious decision not to hide or hold back in any way. The moment is guided by the intentional choice to connect with another on a deep, truly intimate level. As part of this process, each of you must recognize the male/female differences and work with them to achieve authentic and sustainable intimacy.

As I stated before, men and women are very different in how they approach physical intimacy. This creates fertile ground for misunderstandings, hurt feelings, and unmet needs. When each partner's intimacy needs are being met, the magnitude of this issue in the relationship lessens. If one partner's needs are not being met, however, the question of physical intimacy takes on primary importance and receives a disproportionate share of attention. In order for this matter to return to being just one aspect of the relationship instead of its main focus, it is necessary for each partner to understand the needs of the other and to intentionally meet them.

PHYSICAL INTIMACY: MAKING IT WORK

A few years ago *Parade Magazine* ran an article addressing how men could get more sex. It recommended that men do the dishes. I have also heard that if men want to "get lucky" that night, they need to start setting the stage in the morning. It's really almost that simple. Both of these suggestions involve being aware of what the woman is doing and thinking. If a man makes a pass at his partner while she is doing chores, reading, or watching TV, he probably won't get the response he is seeking. He also will probably be met with frequent rejection if he grabs her as she is getting into bed. However, if he takes the time to be loving and attentive to his partner throughout the day and takes some of the tasks off her plate, he will stand a greater chance of getting a green light.

Women have to be more intentional in meeting their partner's needs as well. They must acknowledge that it may take them longer to get in the mood and become more willing to make the effort to get there. A few years ago, some of my female colleagues were discussing this issue. A couple of us stated that if our partners wanted to be intimate and the answer wasn't a definite "no" it would be a "yes." Frequently we would become engaged in the process and be glad of our decision. If not, we looked at it as a gift to our partner. Either way, it brought us closer together as couples. This was because we willingly met our partner's needs, rather than making a concession.

The underlying point is that both of you must make the effort to meet the other's physical intimacy needs. The responsibility of making the relationship work in this important arena falls to you both. When only one partner takes on the responsibility for meeting the physical intimacy needs of the other, the relationship becomes one-sided and, ultimately, vulnerable. But if both of you pay attention to this fundamental aspect of your relationship, and behave with intention toward your partner, the closeness you develop will lovingly sustain your relationship.

FINAL THOUGHTS

Intimacy is an important part of marriage and must be consciously nurtured if you and your partner are to have a successful relationship. Intimacy encompasses both your physical relationship and your emotional connectedness. Marriage is a high-stakes relationship that can be full of anxiety and conflict as you define your *Us* while still holding on to your own identity. Your ability to connect with your partner on a deep, intimate level during this process, and throughout your relationship, will determine its overall health and longevity.

SUGGESTED DESIGN ACTIVITIES

Intimacy plays a huge role in marital success. In fact, having a stable relationship with another that supports our need for intimacy is one of the major reasons people marry. The following questions are designed to help you and your partner build a truly intimate relationship with each other.

1. How do you like to be intimate with your partner? How does your partner like to be intimate with you?

2. How do you shut your partner out? How do you feel shut out from your partner?

3. What challenges do you have sharing intimate thoughts and feelings with your partner? What challenges does your partner have?

4. What challenges do you have being physically intimate with your partner? What challenges does your partner have?

5. What are your concerns about maintaining intimacy with your partner through the years? What are your partner's concerns?

CHAPTER 13
THE SECOND TIME AROUND

Marriage is the triumph of hope over experience.

– Samuel Johnson, author & moralist

Jonathan and Theresa came to see me to address issues in their relationship before they got married. Both had been married before and each has children from those marriages. The eldest two of Jonathan's children are grown and out of the house. His youngest two are both in high school and live with his ex-wife, Joan. There is a visitation schedule but the teens don't always follow it and Joan supports their decision. Theresa has a four-year-old daughter, Anna, who lives with her full-time but has visitation with her father.

Jonathan was married for 20 years to his first wife before he left due to her infidelity. His children, in their ignorance of the facts, blame him for the divorce. He feels guilty for not being able to make that marriage work and, as a result, has great difficulty setting boundaries with Joan and with his children. Still, Jonathan grew up with the *Brady Bunch* as part of his cultural background and believes everything will eventually work out with everyone coming to love, accept, and enjoy each other with time. Theresa is not so sure. Even though Theresa came on the scene well after Jonathan's divorce, she feels that Jonathan's children resent her presence in their father's life. She believes that Jonathan's difficulty in setting limits with his children has left her perpetually in second place. "Family dinners are important to me but Jonathan doesn't even try and make them come to the table to eat. They fill up their plates and head off to the living room to watch TV. They aren't even required to thank me for the meal I prepared," Theresa complained. "I end up feeling like their servant."

Jonathan and Theresa have already had arguments over how and where to spend the holidays, disruptions in their routine when his children decide to visit, Jonathan's financial obligations to his adult children, and the general lack of respect Theresa feels from his ex and his children. Even though Jonathan understands Theresa's feelings and agrees that his children don't always behave as he'd like, he feels he's in a no-win situation whatever he does. "My kids hold all the cards," Jonathan explains. "If I try to make Theresa happy by insisting they follow our rules, the kids just refuse to come over. So I ease up to get them to visit and Theresa feels her desires aren't important. I try to make everyone happy but I just end up making matters worse."

Challenges exist with Theresa's daughter and ex-husband as well. Jonathan tries to help with Anna, but he and Theresa have different parenting styles that lead to disagreements. Her ex, Sam, is also not always reliable with child support and this adds to their financial struggles. So, in addition to the usual challenges facing couples planning to marry, Jonathan and Theresa are struggling with the impact of their "first families."

THE CHALLENGE OF SECOND MARRIAGES

Remarriage presents particular difficulties for couples. In addition to the usual hurdles couples face, remarriage includes finding productive ways to deal with ex-spouses, stepchildren, prior financial obligations, and the constant pull of conflicting emotions and priorities. It means that as part of a second marriage, you have to be even clearer about what you want your marriage to look like and what boundaries you must draw to protect it.

The statistics regarding the success of second and subsequent marriages bear out this challenge. About 65% of remarriages involve children from the prior marriage. Unfortunately, 60% of all remarriages end in divorce, as compared to about 50% for all marriages. This doesn't mean people shouldn't remarry. In fact, about 80% of divorced people remarry. It just means that if you are one of those 80%, you need to go into remarriage with your eyes wide open—not with your fingers crossed like Jonathan.

Success for a remarriage involves all the necessary steps previously discussed for building your *Us*. It also has an additional, and absolutely essential, requirement. This vital step necessitates some serious thinking about what went wrong in your previous marriage. It's very easy to place all of the blame on your ex-spouse, but it won't help you in the long run as you negotiate your new relationship. It's important for you to identify how your own feelings and behavior influenced your previous marriage so that you're less likely to repeat the same mistakes in this one.

I know, you're probably thinking, "But my current partner is *nothing* like the last one." This may be true. However, unless you have gone through this exercise, *you* are the same person you were in your previous relationship. The old adage, "those who do not understand history are doomed to repeat it," applies to relationships as well. The best predictor of future behavior is past behavior. If you have done nothing to examine your previous choices in light of your current relationship, your new marriage may be starting off at a serious disadvantage.

The questions below can help you identify what got in the way of a successful marriage the first time around. As you consider these questions, be sure to address *your* part in the problems, not just those of your ex-spouse.

+ Did the two of you have difficulty defining and/or resolving problems?

+ Did you tend to avoid difficult topics?

+ Did you grow apart? If so, what was your contribution to that?

+ Was there an external event, such as a health crisis or job loss, which you weren't able to negotiate as a team?

+ Did one or both of your families of origin create difficulties for you as a couple? How did you handle these challenges?

+ Was infidelity an issue? If so, do you understand why it happened?

The more you know about yourself and how you react in a committed relationship, the better your chances of success this time around.

If you and your current partner have not addressed these issues, you can be fairly certain that you'll be dealing with them in some shape or form in this new relationship. Problems may not arise in exactly the same way. But if you haven't changed how you react or respond to these types of situations, you will most likely repeat the pattern of behavior that resulted in the difficulties you experienced in your previous marriage. If this is your third or subsequent marriage, the need to go through this exercise of identifying your behavior becomes even more important. The more you know about yourself and how you react in a committed relationship, the better your chances of success this time around.

This is not meant to be an exercise in blame or judgment. Its purpose is solely educational. As Maya Angelou has said, "When we know better, we do better." Marriage requires skills that are different from those of any other relationship. In marriage, you live in intimate proximity to another person of equal stature. Your qualities, good and bad, are on display every day in every conceivable situation. How you handled yourself in your previous relationship, how you responded to your former partner, and how you adapted to being part of a committed couple all provide a roadmap for how you have gotten to where you are now. How well you have learned from that roadmap will influence how successful your current marriage will be. If you come armed with self-knowledge and a plan for what you want this marriage to be, you'll be well on your way to a solid, flourishing relationship.

THE STEPCHILDREN FACTOR

If biological children can have a challenging effect on a marriage, stepchildren can actually be harmful to one. Unlike having a child with your partner and experiencing the changes together, you or your partner already have a relationship with a child that predates the relationship you have with each other. This pre-existing relationship takes time, attention, and resources away from the new relationship you are trying to build. Maneuvering through these issues often involves dealing with strong emotions and divided loyalties. How you and your partner handle each other's biological children can have a profound impact on the success of your marriage. If you harbor any secret hope that your stepchildren will smoothly transition into their new world a la the *Brady Bunch*, let go of it now. If you believe that you can take children from a completely different family with different rules, rituals, history, and traditions and expect them to blend seamlessly with you or other children, you are in for a very rude awakening.

It is more productive to turn your attention to creating a family that focuses on mutual respect, kindness, and acceptance of each person's unique feelings about this new arrangement.

One common reaction to a parent's remarriage is for a child to feel a sense of divided loyalty to the other parent. Look at it from the child's point of view. Your marriage is just as real to them as it is to you, and it changes everything. You are now an everyday part of the child's life instead of just a special friend of their parent.

It is more productive to turn your attention to creating a family that focuses on mutual respect, kindness, and acceptance of each person's unique feelings about this new arrangement.

If there is continuing tension between the child's parents, the child may feel a responsibility to protect the feelings of the parent who has not remarried. The child may view your marriage as a threat to the other parent's happiness and take on the job of defending that person's former position in the family. This may take the form of unfocused anger at any event that doesn't go the child's way, a refusal to participate in "new" family activities, or outright disrespect and defiance to you or your new spouse.

As you enter your new life with stepchildren, you must understand a critical dynamic. With this new marriage, you have shattered the fantasy most children of divorce harbor: the reconciliation of their parents and the return to their former life. While you and your partner are experiencing the joy and excitement a new marriage can bring, the children are staring at the cold, hard reality of the complete destruction of their old life. How you and your partner handle these dichotomous feelings will help set the foundation for the children's acceptance of your marriage and your place in their family.

THE GRIEF OF DIVORCE

Divorce is a loss for everyone involved, and each family member must grieve that loss. One challenge of grief is that everyone goes through it in their own way and on their own timetable. Just because you and/or your partner have processed your own emotions from a previous marriage and are ready to move on doesn't mean your children are similarly ready. While children should not be able to dictate the life choices of their parents, it is deeply disrespectful to not consider their feelings. Ignoring children's feelings is also ultimately not supportive of your new relationship. When children believe their feelings don't matter and that their parent is choosing you over them, that's when the "fun" really begins. Now, everything becomes a battle between you and them. Your partner, their biological parent, will be trapped in the no-man's land of trying to make you both feel like a priority. The resulting stress on your relationship will either destroy your marital bond or seriously undermine your partner's relationship with their child. Neither outcome is acceptable.

Mary came to my office because she was very concerned about her 15-year-old daughter, Nicole. She had been skipping school, lying, hanging out with a 20-year-old guy, and doing cocaine and ecstasy. Mary had divorced Nicole's father five years before, in large part because he was a drug addict. Mary was especially terrified that Nicole had started running away. Mary was worried that if something didn't change—quickly—she would lose her daughter to addiction or the streets. Nicole had told Mary that she would stop running away if she could go live with her dad. Mary didn't like that option because she knew her ex was still using and would establish no boundaries for Nicole. "I'm scared and don't know what to do. I have no idea how things got this bad," Mary said through her tears.

Once I got a bit more background from Mary, I began to

understand why all of this was happening. After three years as a single mom, Mary had married Sam, a man whom she loved and could trust. Within a month of the wedding, she had packed up her daughter and son and moved an hour away to a new house and a new town. Nicole had to change schools, friends, and everything else about her life. To make matters worse, no one had ever asked her if she even wanted to make those changes. Enraged and confused, Mary's sweet, charming daughter began the process of turning into a defiant, unhappy adolescent. Nicole felt like she no longer mattered in her mother's life and began to act accordingly. Mary and Sam had responded to Nicole's behavior by becoming increasingly punitive. It had never occurred to Mary that her daughter might not be as happy with their new life as she was.

Not long after I began seeing Mary, Nicole moved in with her father. While the angry fights, unexplained disappearances, and financial chaos were over for Mary, she still hadn't found any peace of mind. Her worry over her daughter's present safety and future success was still with her every day, undermining her happiness. Mary had found a new life with Sam but was completely unprepared for what that new life would cost her.

In fact, Nicole's behavior was neither uncommon nor unpredictable. She was at a critical age when Mary married Sam. Like many teenagers, Nicole believed she was more grown up than she was. Due to her parent's divorce, she also had been given an elevated role in her family. Nicole had become her mother's confidante as well as helping her raise Nicole's brother. Between her age and her new status in the family, Nicole believed she had the right to be included in decisions that affected the family.

But when her mother married Sam, Nicole suddenly lost her position as her mother's "friend" and was demoted back to childhood. She was angry, hurt, and confused. Each time Mary sided with Sam against her, Nicole felt more alone and angry. This vicious cycle led not to the happy new family Mary had dreamed of, but to a nasty tug-of-war between two people she dearly loved.

WHY STEPPARENTS CAN'T PARENT

Sam and Mary's difficulty with Nicole occurred for many reasons. One of their biggest mistakes was to allow Sam to try to "parent" someone who already had two parents. In their sincere attempt to create a family, Sam and Mary made an error common to many second marriages. They assumed that since Sam was now Mary's husband, he could also step into the role of "Dad" on an everyday basis. The problem with this assumption is that Nicole did not share it. Not by a long shot.

In her view, Sam was an interloper with no authority to impose his rules on her. Sam and Mary, like many couples, never developed a plan for how the new spouse would fit into the existing family hierarchy. They assumed that their recognition of Sam as the man of the house would be automatically accepted. Not so. The older the child, the more likely this assumption will explode into conflict. The reason is simple: your new partner is *not* your child's parent. As discussed above, your child's loyalties will already be tested by your remarriage. Trying to replace a child's parent, no matter how benignly meant, is likely to be met with resistance.

So how, you may ask, can you successfully integrate your new partner into the family? The best way is to develop a clear plan between you and your new partner and then you, as the parent, put it into practice. This plan would include elements such as family rules about chores, homework, and behavioral expectations; family rituals like mealtime, recreational activities, and vacations; and clear guidelines for family roles and appropriate hierarchy. Since you are the common bond between old and new, you are the only person who can pull off this shift with any hope of success.

In addition, you'll need to include your children in age-appropriate ways if you want to minimize their resistance. They can have input into when chores are done, what type of recreational activities they want to participate in, and in setting the family rules. You have to remember that your children are trying to cope with all the changes that have occurred in their lives. They may not be at the same level of acceptance, and it's important that you and your partner meet them where they are. It may be difficult knowing they may not share your sense of happiness at this point, but if their feelings are acknowledged and accepted, the chance for a peaceful existence goes up.

When people with children from previous relationships get together, the *Us* they form must take into account those children. Unlike couples whose children come later, your *Us* must be ready to accommodate the constant presence of others from day one. If you and your partner have not defined a clear plan, you will constantly be reacting to what's going on with the children instead of actively managing your home life. And remember, it's not just about what *you* think will work best. You also must understand what changes your partner sees as essential for your relationship to flourish, given the constraints the children bring.

Once all this is negotiated, defined, and put into practice, what, then, is the role of a stepparent? Their role becomes one of what I call "adulting." Adulting is what any person in a role of authority can do with respect to a child's behavior. Whether you are a babysitter, teacher, neighbor, or stepparent, if you are aware of the rules of the house and are present when those rules are being violated, then you act as any adult would and remind the child of what is acceptable behavior. If the child doesn't respond, and is not in imminent danger, then you bring the misbehavior to the attention of the parent and let them mete out any disciplinary action. As an additional adult in the family, you have the role of backing your partner in carrying out the rules, but not initiating any consequences. That is the only way to effectively balance the power between you and the children.

As a new person in the lives of the children, you can play an extraordinary role in their lives. You can be a role model, a mentor, and/or a special friend. Because you are not related to them, and therefore don't *have* to care about them, choosing to take an active role in their lives can have a truly positive impact on them. You can give them something neither of their parents can: an adult who cares about them because they want to, not because they have to.

HANDLING THE EXES

When Susan and Michael married, they had already been together for ten years and had an 8-year-old son, Jeff. Their marriage lasted less than two years. Michael was somewhat self-absorbed and only spent time with Jeff when they did something that Michael wanted to do. However, once the couple split, he demanded visitation rights. He expected Susan to follow the letter of the custody agreement even though he regularly skipped child support payments and had never paid Susan her part of the divorce settlement. In addition, Michael was always late picking up or dropping off Jeff for scheduled visits.

When Susan got involved with a new man, Bruce, shortly after the separation, Michael's behavior became worse. He would tell Jeff what an awful mother Susan was and that she loved Bruce more than Jeff. Michael would never take his son places Jeff wanted to go, telling him that his mother had taken all the money he otherwise happily would have spent on the child. Whenever Michael found out that Susan had special plans on the weekends he had their son, he would concoct some emergency that would keep him from having the visitation. He would then demand to have Jeff the next weekend, even though he was the one who had altered the schedule.

Susan had never learned to stand up to Michael during their marriage, and she continued to follow that pattern. Bruce was getting more and more frustrated by Michael's continued interference in his relationship with Susan. Michael would call to talk to Jeff during dinner and after his son's bedtime. When Susan or Bruce told him that he couldn't talk to his son at these inconvenient times, Michael would angrily demand to be allowed access to his child or he would take them to court.

When the police did show up at Bruce's workplace one day with a restraining order taken out by Michael, Bruce successfully fought the order but could not undo the embarrassment it had caused. Just after Bruce and Susan set a wedding date, Michael filed a challenge to get full custody, claiming negligence due to parental alienation. At this point, Bruce and Susan came to me for help in saving their relationship.

Dealing effectively with an ex is an ongoing reality that cannot be wished away. While Susan and Bruce's experience with Michael may be extreme, it is unlikely that you and your partner can happily share a vacation cottage with your ex, their partner, and the kids, a la Bruce Willis and Demi Moore. The more likely scenario is one in which you negotiate and renegotiate ceasefires. If either you or your partner has not made peace with your emotions related to the previous marriage, these ceasefires will probably be short-lived. If the ex can continue to push your buttons, they have the capacity to ruin your new relationship.

If you have been married before and your former spouse is still in the picture, it's your job to protect your new relationship from untoward behavior by that ex. In order to do this effectively, you need to manage your own behavior. If you still are engaging in unproductive patterns with your ex, you need to learn what your part of the pattern is and learn to deal with your former spouse in a different way. Just as you could not change your ex while you were married, you cannot change what your ex does now.

The only thing you *can* change is how you respond to their behavior. If you respond in the same old way, you will be putting your new relationship in harm's way. You and your new partner get to decide how the two of you want to allow your ex in your life, but you are the one who must enforce those boundaries. Like Michael, your ex may call you at inconvenient times, causing disruption in your life. You may choose to let the phone call go to voicemail instead of answering immediately. You can then return the call when it is more convenient. This would only be done after you had informed your ex of the new rules.

While the partner with the ex has the role of intermediary between the two families, the new partner has an important role to play as well. You knew your partner was once married. If there are children from that marriage, your partner's ex has a right to be involved in their lives. This means that person will be involved in yours. Pretending otherwise, or making it difficult for your partner to have a productive relationship with their ex, will have a negative impact on your marriage.

It is completely fair to share your opinion on how your partner interacts with their ex as it relates to your own relationship. However, you cannot demand your partner do things your way. You may be right that your partner's ex purposely does things to interfere in your life, but holding your partner accountable for what their ex chooses to do is unproductive. The more you and your partner react to the ex, the more power you give them over your life. By contrast, the better the two of you handle the influence of the ex, the greater your chances for a successful and enduring relationship.

THE EXTENDED *Us*

When you marry someone who is divorced, and especially if they have children, your *Us* starts from a different place than for those who have never been married. Instead of being able to take your time establishing your foundation of togetherness and then carefully crafting space for children, you have to make room for children from the get-go. This is akin to living in a house while you are trying to build it. It requires the ability to keep the greater vision in mind while maintaining the flexibility to handle the immediate challenges associated with lack of space, time, and amenities.

Because the process of defining the *Us* is more complex in a second marriage, you may be tempted to cut corners or put off the hard decisions until later. Don't. Whatever measures you put in place in the beginning of your relationship will tend to take root. Unless you are very diligent in identifying what is a temporary fix and make a specific plan to address it, inertia can take over. More than likely, you'll find that what you planned to be temporary has become a permanent part of your relationship.

So, start right out of the gate. Be proactive in distinguishing what belongs to the two of you and what can be expanded to include the children. Become clear about the role any exes will play. Once you mutually define the boundaries of your *Us*, the job of presenting them to the world becomes easier. Each of you needs to be certain that you aren't making concessions to the situation, but rather are making real accommodations. Remember, if you don't take the time at the beginning to put your relationship first, you will be leaving it vulnerable to the demands of the interested others.

As part of your *Us*, you and your partner get to decide the rules of the house and how those rules apply to any children who live there. This can be challenging if the children live in your household sporadically. It can be especially problematic if the rules in your house are very different from those in their other home.

Once again, be sure that both of you are making accommodations, not concessions. If there is any disagreement between the two of you, it must be worked out before involving the children. (Use the tools for productive conversations outlined in Chapter 11.) Any discrepancy in understanding, no matter how small, can be used by the children to create confusion and discord. Once the two of you have reached consensus, it is the job of the biological parent to introduce and implement the rules. You can present this in a family meeting with both of you present, but the parent must take the lead.

In creating your *Us,* you and your partner also must carve out time for yourselves as well. You will have to be very intentional about this because of so many other demands on your time. However, if you don't make this a priority, no one else will. No matter how crazy or hectic things get in a household with children moving back and forth and exes making demands, you and your partner have to build in time for rituals, dating, and alone time. Some couples do this on the "off" weekends when the children are with the other parent. This isn't necessarily a bad option as long as you also make some time to be together when the children are with you. That's because it's important for them to see you as a couple, not just two adults in charge of the house.

FINAL THOUGHTS

Like first-time married couples, you need to create an *Us* for your remarriage that will guide your decisions and behavior as a team. But unlike other couples, you don't get to gradually introduce other people into that *Us.* Biological children don't know any other family but the one they're born into. Children who come into second marriages come with a history of another family. Their other parent shows up in your new marriage, too. Everyone arrives with their own feelings and agendas. You and your partner need to be prepared for those challenges. A solid, well-defined *Us* will enable you to handle those demands from others while keeping your relationship healthy and productive.

SUGGESTED DESIGN ACTIVITIES

Second, and subsequent, marriages have challenges that are different from first marriages. The following questions are meant to help you and your partner avoid many of the pitfalls remarriage brings.

1. What do you think caused your first marriage to end? What caused your partner's first marriage to end?

2. What have you done to address your part in the difficulties that arose in your first marriage? What has your partner done?

3. What are you going to do differently in this marriage to ensure its success?

4. If you have children, do you know how they feel about your new relationship? Have you been able to accept your children's feelings and make accommodations for them?

5. How have you and your partner planned to fit the children into your relationship? How have you planned to manage the exes?

CHAPTER 14

CREATING AN INTENTIONAL MARRIAGE

*Marriage is that relation between man and woman
in which the independence is equal, the
dependence mutual, and the obligation reciprocal.*

– Louis K. Anspacher, playwright

If you have gotten to this point in the book, first I must thank you for your patience and perseverance, two qualities that will serve you well in your marriage. Second, you clearly know by now that your wedding was only the down payment on your "happily ever after." To keep your relationship strong, it is essential that you find a way to take the tradition of marriage—with all of its history, customs, and expectations—and make it uniquely yours. This means you'll need to put some thought and planning into what you and your partner really want your marriage to be, and not merely place your faith in love alone.

I hope you have come to see you have the power to raise your odds for a happy, successful marriage. By understanding and implementing the principles and tools introduced in previous chapters, you can take ownership of your relationship and shape it into something vital and enduring. The "happily ever after" you seek can be yours. The result you get will be determined by your own beliefs and, most importantly, your actions.

ACTING WITH INTENTION

Few couples expect that they'll be anything less than happy in their marriages. It's not as though couples wake up one day and decide they're miserable together and their marriage is over. It happens gradually and without intent. But happiness in marriage *is* a choice. Thoughts become actions. You make decisions based on the information you choose to pay attention to. Emotions play their part by helping you understand your perspective on what you are experiencing. What you think, feel, and do all come into alignment. You truly do create your own reality.

Happiness in marriage
is **a choice.**

Whether you think your relationship is happy or not, you are correct, because you will focus on the thoughts and actions that support your view. If you chose to focus on *you*, what *you're* getting and what's happening that makes *you* upset in the relationship, you are going to create problems. This is because you are forgetting that you asked someone to walk through life with you and it no longer is just about you. This is the very foundation of the concept of the *Us*.

However, if you focus on your partner and what makes them feel happy and loved, it will come back to you. This is the basis of both the "pay it forward" concept and the law of attraction. What you put out into the world, you will receive back. It really works. When you meet your partner's needs with intention, you increase the probability that your needs will be met because you're making your partner feel cared for and valued. Again, this is not to say your needs aren't important—they are. This is about where you choose to focus your attention.

Couples often enter into a relationship with the fantasy that their partner will somehow "complete" them. But a more productive goal is to work together to complete your *Us*. The concept of the *Us* is based on the idea that the whole is greater than the sum of its parts. You don't complete each other; you complete a greater whole. When you create the *Us,* you and your partner surrender to your marriage, to the greater relationship. You are in no way submitting *to* your partner, but rather working *with* them to create a workable and loving life plan. Acting intentionally in your marriage should create an ongoing "battle of generosity" between the two of you. The challenge: Who can do more for the other?

THE *US* AS MARITAL SUPERGLUE

Over time, marriage has become less of a social institution and more of a voluntary lifestyle—one that can be chosen and then unchosen. As one of my clients recently realized, relationships don't just happen naturally. But most people go into marriage without a plan. When they run into the inevitable bumps, they have no guidelines to help them find a way through. This book is meant to help you to intentionally create a plan for your marriage—a blueprint, if you will—that will allow you and your partner to navigate life's bumps with your love and relationship intact.

This plan is grounded in taking the time to get to know each other and, then, jointly deciding that you're willing to put in the time, energy, and attention a marriage requires. It requires that each of you is happy with the other person as they are *right now*. You have also discussed all aspects of marriage—emotional, financial, domestic, familial—and understand and accept each other's views.

While neither of you is making concessions about what is important to you, both of you are able to make accommodations that support your collective view of the relationship. You understand that neither of you is responsible for the other's happiness, but you try hard to bring out the best in each other. You recognize that there will be bumps in the road, but you're willing to make the commitment to navigate those bumps together. You understand that marriage is about more than love. It's about building a life together.

Marriage is the relationship that embodies the persistent pull between the two life forces of togetherness and separateness. These twin needs create an ongoing tug of war that requires you to find a delicate balance between being your own person and being part of a larger community. It is this personal struggle that led me to the concept of the *Us*. The *Us* creates the stabilizing third leg of the triangle between you and your partner, bringing safety and security to a marriage. It is an idea that finds expression in the candle ceremony of many weddings. The bride and groom each hold an individual light and then join them together. They don't extinguish their own lights but create a brighter light that will guide them through any future darkness.

The creation of your *Us* is an ongoing journey, not a destination. It is a lifelong process. How patiently and skillfully you design, build, and maintain your relationship will determine how vital and enduring it will be. If you pay close attention and treat your marriage with the loving care it deserves, your "happily ever after" marriage will be like a castle that has withstood time and the elements, remaining strong and beautiful.

FINAL THOUGHTS

When I started this endeavor, my dream was to help couples like you stay out of trouble and create lasting love. Hopefully, the concept of the *Us* and the tools I have presented in this book have helped you and your partner acquire a better understanding of how to create the marriage you imagined. The ideas are simple in concept but not necessarily easy to implement. The examples and exercises throughout the book were designed to help you begin this lifelong process.

However, this doesn't mean that your marital journey will always be free of challenges. If you have questions or challenges, I would like to stay in touch with you. Please feel free to visit my website (www.blueprintforalastingmarriage.com) for further assistance. I will continue to provide information and opportunities to help keep your marriage strong and happy.

Additionally, when you visit the site you'll receive an invitation to a free, live teleseminar to get further information to help you and your partner build your dream relationship. I also invite you to share your success stories on the site, and to read those of others.

In the meantime, I wish you and your partner the very best on your life journey together.

Bibliography

Arbinger Institute. (2000) *Leadership and Self-Deception: Getting Out of the Box.* Berrett-Koehler Publishers, Inc. San Francisco, CA.

Chapman, Gary D. (1992) *The Five Love Languages: The Secret to Love that Lasts.* Northfield Publishing. Chicago, IL.

Doherty, William. (2001) *Take Back Your Marriage: Sticking Together in a World That Pulls Us Apart.* The Guilford Press. New York, NY.

Gottmann, John. (1994) *Why Marriages Succeed or Fail: And How You Can Make Yours Last.* Simon and Schuster, New York, NY.

Gray, John. (1992) *Men are from Mars, Women are from Venus: The Classic Guide to Understanding the Opposite Sex.* Harper-Collins Publishers. New York, NY.

Harley, Willard F., Jr. (1986) *His Needs, Her Needs: Building an Affair-Proof Marriage.* Fleming H. Revell. Grand Rapids, MI.

Harley, Willard F., Jr. (1988) *Marriage Insurance: Building a Divorce-proof Marriage.* Fleming H. Revell Co. Old Tappan, NJ.

Hargrave, Terry. (2000) *The Essential Humility of Marriage: Honoring the Third Identity in Couple Therapy.* Zeig, Tucker, & Theisen, Inc. Redding, CT.

Maslow, Abraham. (1954) *Motivation and Personality.* Harper-Collins Publishers. New York, NY.

Perel, Ester. (2006) *Mating in Captivity: Unlocking Erotic Intelligence.* HarperCollins Publishers. New York, NY .

Tannen, Deborah. (2001) *I Only Say This Because I Love You: How the Way We Talk Can Make or Break Family Relationships Throughout Our Lives.* Random House. New York, NY.

ACKNOWLEDGMENTS

Being a writer was never something I aspired to, mostly because I never thought it was something I could do. There are many people who have crossed my path who believed otherwise. First and foremost would be Bill O'Hanlon, who generously encouraged me to begin this journey. Second would be Anne Hartree, my first business coach and friend, who helped me to see the possibilities and have the courage to be ready for opportunities.

There are many others whose valuable assistance kept me on track and moving forward through this extended process. John Eggen and Lorna McLeod of Mission Marketing Mentors provided much of the nuts and bolts necessary for getting the book completed. I also owe a debt of gratitude to David Harris, my accountability partner, for holding my feet to the fire and seeing me through to the end. I want to thank my content editors: Robin Quinn, who helped shape the overall structure of the book, and Marian Sandmaier for her honest critique of the manuscript and invaluable suggestions for improvements. I also owe a huge debt of gratitude to my long-time coach Casey Truffo for helping me to grow outside my therapy office.

My family—my husband, Steve, son, Drew, and daughter, Jenna—are especially appreciated for their patience and encouragement over the last year. They have put up with late dinners, less than stellar housekeeping, and time spent with my computer instead of them. Without their love and support, no endeavor in my life would have any meaning.

Finally, I owe special gratitude to the many couples who trusted me with their life stories and hopes for better relationships. I have been honored to be an intimate part of your lives. You have given me as much, if not more, than I have been able to return. That which you have taught me about marriage is what I strive to pass on to others. Thank you for your generosity.